❧ NOTHING IS LOST

The Lockert Library of Poetry in Translation

Editorial Advisor: Richard Howard

FOR OTHER TITLES IN THE LOCKERT LIBRARY, SEE PAGE 165

Edvard Kocbek

NOTHING IS LOST

Selected Poems

Edited and with an Introduction by
Michael Scammell

Translated by
Michael Scammell *and* Veno Taufer

Foreword by Charles Simic

PRINCETON UNIVERSITY PRESS

PRINCETON AND OXFORD

Published by Princeton University Press, 41 William Street,
Princeton, New Jersey 08540
In the United Kingdom: Princeton University Press, 3 Market Place, Woodstock,
Oxfordshire oX20 1SY

Library of Congress Cataloging-in-Publication Data

Kocbek, Edvard.
[Poems. English. Selections]
Nothing is lost : selected poems / Edvard Kocbek ; edited and with an introduction
by Michael Scammell ; translated by Michael Scammell and Veno Taufer ; foreword
by Charles Simic.
    p. cm. — (The Lockert library of poetry in translation)
Translated from Slovenian.
ISBN 0-691-11839-6 (cloth : alk. paper) — ISBN 0-691-11840-X (pbk. : alk. paper)
1. Kocbek, Edvard—Translations into English.   I. Scammell, Michael.   II. Taufer,
Veno, 1933–   III. Title.   IV. Series.

PG1918.K58A27 2004
891.8'415—dc22   2003062203

Britsh Library Cataloging-in-Publication Data is available

This book has been composed in Postscript Trump Typeface
Printed on acid-free paper. ∞
www.pupress.princeton.edu

Printed in the United States of America

10 9 8 7 6 5 4 3 2 1

The Lockert Library of Poetry in Translation is supported by a bequest from Charles
Lacy Lockert (1888–1974)

Contents

FOREWORD *by Charles Simic*   ix

ACKNOWLEDGMENTS   xiii

INTRODUCTION *by Michael Scammell*   1

From EARTH   13

Silent birds perch on my shoulders   15
The sun is wreathed in cobwebs   17
A pair of strong young oxen goes slowly   19
The women are coming from work   21
The heavy bole presses the last basket of grapes   23
O noise of waters, collapse of the universe   25
Loud greetings to you, my living comrades   27
Drunk with change I lie on the ground   29
Earth, I get everything from you   31

From DREAD   33

Rain   35
Hands   37
Moonlight   39
Moon with a Halo   41
Crucifix in a Field   43
The Game   45
After the Meeting   47
Unknown Woman   49
The Bay   51
Night Ritual   53
Midnight Wind   55
Dialectics   57
Black Sea   59
The Stick   61

Grace   63
Landscape   65
Migration   67
Things   69
Summons   71
Presentiment   73
Prayer   75

From PENTAGRAM   77

On Night Watch   79
Doubled   81
How Shall I Be?   83
Pentagram   85
The Cave   87
Image in Old Bark   89
Night Doffs Its Weapons   91

From REPORT   93

Parrots   95
Contraband   97
Exercise   99
Girl's Apron   101
Climax   103
Ditty   105
Now   107
Pontic   109
The Game Is Over   111
Play Backwards   113
Longing for Jail   115
My Partisan Name   117
Lippizaners   119

From EMBERS   125

Tree   127
What Happens to the Mountain   129

Unknown Beloved   131
The Time of the Poem   133
Blessed Search   135

From BRIDE IN BLACK   137

Amok   139
What We Were Looking For   141
The Statue   143
Tongue   145
Plea   147
Stammer, Children   149
Girl   151
On Freedom of Mind   153
Ancient Miracle   155
The Generosity of the Poem   157
Now We Are Alone   159
Game   161
I haven't done playing with words   163

Foreword

INVISIBLE FOOTPRINTS ON THE CEILING

ONE of the major literary events of the last forty years is the discovery of East European poetry in the West. Before that, it was the French, and to a lesser extent German, Spanish, and South American poetries that occupied poets and astute readers in England and the United States. All that changed in the 1960s with the publication of Czeslaw Milosz's anthology *Postwar Polish Poetry*, Penguin's series of individual volumes of Modern European Poets, and scores of other translations. In addition to Milosz, names of previously unknown, but clearly major figures such as Zbigniew Herbert, Vladimir Holan, Yannis Ritsos, Osip Mandelstam, Wisława Szymborska, Miroslav Holub, Attila Jozsef, Vasko Popa, and a good number of others were beginning to be known and read. It wasn't just the high quality and originality of their poetry that attracted readers. Here were poets who had had firsthand experience of evil, who lived through wars, revolutions, mass slaughter, various occupations, years of oppression, and came through not only with their moral and aesthetic values intact, but even with their sense of humor preserved. They seemed to have been better witnesses of our barbaric age than poets elsewhere, more savvy about how nationalist and utopian projects work in practice and more likely to speak truth to power. By the early 1990s it appeared to us who pay close attention to such things that every poet of worth in that part of the world had been accounted for, that there were no other happy discoveries to be made. Having read Edvard Kocbek years before in Serbian translation, I knew better. An important poet had been lost sight of.

It's not difficult to find an explanation for that. When one writes in a language spoken by a little more than two million people, the number of translators and opportunities to publish abroad are not many. In Kocbek's case, it took Michael Scammell's and Veno Taufer's love for the poetry and perseverance over many years to remedy this neglect. There may be another reason for him being so little known. His life story is somewhat different from that of the poets I mentioned. He fought with the Communists in World War II, became an important figure in the new government and ended up living in virtual house arrest after publishing some war diaries that readily admitted his side also committed war crimes. Even as a poet, Kocbek is not easily classifiable. He is an unapologetic regionalist, a pastoral poet, a writer of lyrics, and then, of course, he's much more than that. His poems have plenty to do with what happened to him and yet, with a few exceptions, there's little overtly autobiographical about them. The first person pronoun we encounter is more likely to represent a sensibility, a moral consciousness, and a view of the world rather than a person detailing the events of his life. Kocbek is a connoisseur of philosophical paradoxes and impossible moral predicaments. Here's the beginning of his poem "Hands"

> *I have lived between my two hands*
> *as between two brigands,*
> *neither knew*
> *what the other did.*
> *The left hand was foolish because of its heart,*
> *the right hand was clever because of its skill,*
> *one took, the other lost,*
> *they hid from one another*
> *and left everything half-finished.*

History versus nature, reality versus free play of the imagination, freedom versus necessity, and the fine line where they meet is his constant concern. He reminds me of Wallace Stevens in that his ideas, too, had to be constantly subjected to dialectical inquiry in the light of fresh experience. He refused to be pigeonholed either as a man or as a poet. Stubborn defiance of all dogmas was what he believed in. "The law of freedom of the human mind," he said in another poem, "is like the quiet defense of ancient rights."

And yet for all his fascination with ideas, Kocbek is not an intellectual poet. "I have been lowered into the depths / of foolish history," he says in a poem. He is too much interested in the fates of others to be just that. "Once I was you and you me," he writes. Nor does he regard himself as guiltless. He, too, took part in that bloody history. Kocbek started out as a pastoral poet, a pantheist of sorts, and then history rumbled through his beloved landscape. This is his subject. First it was war that made men into heroes and killers, and then it was Communism which made them into hypocrites and liars. In the poem "Dialectics" the daughter of the man next door is an informer who keeps a microphone under the bed. Her father suffers a stroke, the microphone's current fails, and the daughter goes to confession. Even for her Kocbek has compassion. He says: "Everyone clings to a ram's belly / when sneaking from the Cyclops' cave."

What stands out for me in this extraordinary collection of poems is not just the number of truly great poems, but the exquisiteness of Kocbek's lyric voice, the beauty of his phrasing and his images. This is all due, of course, to the fine work of his translators who have done what always seems to me to verge on impossibility. They have preserved the music and the eloquence of the original in the translations.

> *Earth, our grave, how lovely you are, earth,*
> *I am a sweet dark grain among grains, bewildered*
> *by your depths, birds chirrup over our heads,*
> *one of them will peck us up.*

In the end, what surprised me the most about this poem is his mysticism, which had a fairly familiar Christian context in his early poems, but became more philosophical in his later work. I'm thinking of that long tradition which begins with Parmenides who posed the question, why is there something rather than nothing, and concludes with Heidegger and his speculation about the nature of being and nothingness. For Kocbek, the deepest essence of things, too, is *something* for which there is no word, which exists merely as a blessed presentiment, something, he says, that is constantly on the other side, but is nevertheless always with me. If only the ineffable and the inexplicable are genuinely true, then one is allowed to go for broke. "Invisible footprints on the ceiling," he writes in a poem "Exercise." It's crazy, but it sounds right. Simply said, Kocbek's poetry is the work of the most exquisite poetic imagination. These fine translations introduce us to a poet who belongs in company of some of the best and most familiar names in modern poetry.

CHARLES SIMIC

Acknowledgments

ALL THE POEMS in this selection (with the exception of "I haven't done playing with words," which remained unfinished at the time of the poet's death) are taken from Edvard Kocbek, *Zbrane Pesmi* (Selected Poems), vols. 1 and 2 (Cankarjeva Založba, Ljubljana, 1977) to whose publisher acknowledgment is made.

Some of these translations appeared earlier in *Modern Poetry in Translation, No. 8* (1970); Vasa Mihajlovic, editor, *Contemporary Yugoslav Poetry* (Iowa, 1977); and the *New York Review of Books*, October 24, 1991.

Introduction

EDVARD KOCBEK was born in 1904 in the foothills of the southeastern Alps in a part of the world that is now Slovenia, but at that time was still Austria, and thus part of the Austro-Hungarian empire. His father was an organist at the local Roman Catholic church, and Kocbek spent so much time helping him that he later described the church as his second home. In high school he studied classics and foreign languages, and by the time he had finished his schooling, World War I had come and gone and left Slovenia with limited independence as part of the newly established Kingdom of the Serbs, Croats, and Slovenes. Kocbek entered the Catholic seminary in Slovenia's second city, Maribor, with the intention of becoming a priest, but after two years left in protest against the rigid rules and narrow outlook of his clerical superiors. It was a sign of things to come, yet despite this early and characteristic rebellion against orthodoxy, he did not lose his faith. "A person's essence," he wrote in his essay "Thoughts on Man" some ten years later, "lies in the conscious and ceaseless realization of God's creative presence in him;" and he continued to practice a highly personal brand of Catholicism till the end of his life.

Moving from Maribor to Ljubljana, the capital of Slovenia, Kocbek studied Romance languages and literature at the university and edited the Catholic youth magazine, *Cross*, while also contributing poems and articles to a Catholic Socialist periodical called *Fire*. As a promising young poet, he attempted to negotiate a middle way between the pious provincialism of much Slovene literature of the time, the avantgarde constructivism pioneered by the poet Srečko Kosovel, and the self-conscious documentary realism associated with the popularity of socialism. Of crucial importance for his development were two trips to western Europe, one to spend a summer in Berlin, and another on a year's scholarship to France, where he encountered German expressionism and French surrealism first hand, and came under the influence of Emmanuel Mounier and his circle at the Catholic literary magazine, *Esprit*. Mounier had developed a brand of radical Christian socialism that he called "Personalism," which rejected the idealist notion that men's activities were no more than a reflection of the spirit, and accepted that religion did not hold all the answers to the social problems of the modern world.

Returning to Slovenia, Kocbek wrote an outstanding cycle of poems, "Autumn Poems" in a mode that might be described as metaphysical realism: a religious response to the natural world was combined with an attempt to reconcile the spiritual essence of life with physical appearances. In most of these poems Kocbek ignored traditional rhyme and meter in favor of free verse forms shaped by rhythm and assonance, and introduced a modernist aesthetic to a poetry dominated by folklore and romanticism. Building on this cycle, Kocbek went on to produce several more cycles ("Love Poems," "Comrade Poems," "Poems about the Earth") that he brought together in his aptly named first collection of verse, *Earth*, in 1934, a work that set the seal on his growing reputation as Slovenia's most original and accomplished young poet.

The poems in *Earth* were set in his native region of eastern Slovenia, a land of low rolling hills, vineyards, wine presses, pastures, and wooded hills that was intimately familiar to him from his childhood, and they evoke a settled world of peaceful work and play in the pastoral tradition.

> *The sun is wreathed in cobwebs,*
> *the air is homely, as in a curtained*
> *cottage parlor, and a heavy fruit*
> *has rolled downhill into the rotting wood.*
> *Now and then a wheelbarrow squeaks,*
> *there is a sudden rustle in the long leaves*
> *of corn, and the lazy hum of late bees*
> *over the buckwheat.*

It is a world in which men and women take their place as an integral part of nature, whether it be peasant women climbing the fields on their way home from work in the evening, or men slipping into sleep by the wine presses after a day spent crushing the grapes. The poet, "an ancient monk" watching "the enchanted world" before him, maintains his vigil while others sleep.

Stars twinkle outside,
then the lamp burns low, the dripping stops, and
for a long time there is nothing, until, down in the valley,
the morning bell tolls.

The poet's sympathies extend to the animal kingdom too. In one much celebrated poem Kocbek describes a drover and his team of oxen "moving with measured jerks" as they slowly cross a landscape and disappear behind some trees.

Their glistening russet hides smell warm,
and as they enter the wood with their dreamy
driver, it seems they are disappearing forever.

A little later I see the young red oxen
nodding out of the wood and up the hill.
They haven't changed a bit. In this peaceful
land time has stopped.

There was a hint of pantheism in Kocbek's devotion to nature, mixed with cosmic pain ("Earth, I get everything from you, earth / to you I return, my flesh smells of holy / sacrifice and mortal sorrow . . ."). As he watches the women coming from work he experiences a similar emotion: ". . . their song echoes in the / woods, and I could stuff my mouth with bitter soil / in sorrow over their sound." Lying among a tree's roots as a violent thunderstorm brings premonitions of death, he treasures the thought of his mortality. "Let everything be destroyed except dread / wherein lies intimacy, intimacy."

Kocbek's was a personal horror akin to a kind of holy dread (the Slovenian word *groza*, usually translated as "horror," can equally be rendered as "dread"). This was in line with the philosophy of personal responsibility that he developed in essays on Kierkegaard and Péguy, among others. Only man, he wrote in another essay, could be the source of meaning and "vital fertility," because "in nonpersonal life we find neither well-being, nor order, nor a combination of sense and utility. . . . Man represents a heterogeneous reality in a homogeneous being, he cannot be exhausted spiritually, physically, or socially. . . . The problem of man is in the final analysis a religious problem."

But Kocbek was by no means indifferent to the social and political currents of his time, and was acutely aware of other sorts of horror at large in the world in the mid-thirties. The Kingdom of the Serbs, Croats, and Slovenes, for example, had become a monarchist dictatorship with the new name of Yugoslavia, and an unsavory penchant for political assassinations. Mussolini had come to power in neighboring Italy; Hitler's stentorian threats were being borne on the prevailing winds from the other side of the Alps; and in slightly more distant Spain a civil war had broken out in which the European powers were fighting by proxy, and the twin ideologies of Fascism and Communism had begun their battle for supremacy.

In timid, conformist Slovenia, where the religious and political establishments listened to the Vatican and sided with Franco, Kocbek caused a sensation with an essay, "Reflections on Spain," that he published in 1937 in the Catholic journal, *Home and World*. By serving Fascism, he wrote, the church in Spain was revealing its inherent bias in favor of the "spiritual bourgeoisie." The only recourse for honest dissenters was to risk heresy by demonstrating their "spiritual bravery" and voting for "a greater and better truth according to their consciences." This was far better than supporting the rank hypocrisy with which the church justified Franco's excesses. The essay split the intelligentsia in Slovenia for months afterward, and Kocbek got the punishment he had anticipated when he was indeed accused of heresy and threatened with excommunication.

Kocbek was moving closer to socialism, but saw that it too was an ideology like any other, carrying dangers of its own. "A revolutionary thrust solely for the sake of establishing authority, order, safety and decorum, without a deeper goal, is more likely to decline into petty bourgeois philistinism than to relax into a spiritual entity," he wrote in one of his essays, and in 1941, on the very eve of war, he noted in his literary journal *Act*: "The intellectual of today must understand that much depends on his resoluteness. He must opt for a new order as soon as possible, but must not support any particular ideological group completely. He should remain a free agent within it, a creative center of vital experience."

When war did come to Slovenia, Kocbek did not hestitate. He volunteered at once to join the Executive Committee of the Slovenian Liberation Front, a coalition of resistance forces that included both Tito's Communists and Slovenia's Christian Socialists, whose leader he became, and he rose rapidly within its ranks even after Tito's party had taken more or less complete control. In 1943 he went with the Slovenian delegation to Jajce for the second meeting of the Anti-Fascist Council of the Liberation Movement of Yugoslavia, chaired by Tito, and played a prominent role in the Slovenian resistance to Fascist occupation right up until the war's end. By then this decidedly unmilitary poet had attained the rank of general, and for a brief moment served as a minister in Belgrade, before returning to Ljubljana to become Vice President of the Presidium of the National Assembly of Slovenia and Vice President of the Executive Committee of the Slovenian Liberation Front. He was by far the most senior and most important non-communist in the Slovenian government.

Kocbek did not stop writing during the war years, but nor was he quick to publish after the war ended. The establishment of Communism in the whole of Yugoslavia coincided with a new wave of Stalinism in Russia; the institution of an iron discipline and rigid censorship in Marshall Tito's quasi-independent Yugoslavia was no better than in the Soviet-conquered countries of Central and Eastern Europe. It was not until after Tito broke with the Comintern in 1948 that Kocbek ventured to publish his first postwar book, *Comradeship*, which contained not poetry, but excerpts from his war diaries (1949). The book met with a hostile reception and quickly disappeared from bookshop shelves. Kocbek's unsparing account of some of the excesses of the Communist-led Partisans during the war, including the cold-blooded execution of a group of former prisoners-of-war for refusing to join the Partisans, was too much for Slovenia's leaders to stomach, and the censorship prevented any reprints.

It was Kocbek's book of short stories, *Fear and Courage,* published in 1951, that brought about his public disgrace and official downfall. The book contained four novellas on the Partisans' wartime campaigns and depicted guerrilla warfare with unsparing honesty, encompassing both its bloody heroism and the senseless cruelties endemic to irregular campaigns. Kocbek did not hesitate to confront his own complicity in these actions and expressed his ethical qualms with an objectivity and realism that had not been seen in Slovenian (or Yugoslav) literature before. It was too much for the Yugoslav Communist Party, which in domestic policies was fully in tune with the Stalinism that it professed to reject. Kocbek's book was anathematized as "political pornography" and immediately suppressed. The entire literary and political establishment was mobilized to vilify and denounce him as an enemy of the people, and he was speedily expelled from all his public offices and forced into silence.

For ten years he became a nonperson. His house was watched, his telephone tapped, and he was kept in enforced quarantine. The predictable result of this persecution (particularly in such a small country) was to turn him into a hero to dissidents and a beacon to a younger generation of poets, so that when a few of his poems did begin to appear again, he became a rallying point for the student radicals of the sixties, and the the patron saint of rebellious literary magazines such as *Review-57* and *Perspectives* (both of which were closed by the authorities). Kocbek, meanwhile, earned his living by translating from French and German and publishing the results under a pseudonym. In 1963, virtually thirty years after his last collection, Kocbek was allowed to publish a new book of poems, *Dread*, that included selections from his writings over the preceding decades. The book was a huge success and won the Prešeren Prize (Slovenia's most prestigious literary award) in 1964.

While it was clear that the book's title had a very broad range of meanings, Kocbek was at pains to play down any political overtones and emphasize the personal. *"Dread,"* he explained, "is not just an accidental and unusual title for my second collection of poetry, but is also the reflection of the fundamental atmosphere of my life; dread comprises both wonder and opposition, my dread is pure ecstasy, the continuous possibility of conquering despair and nothingness." Nevertheless, while it remained true that, as in everything he wrote, Kocbek filtered his subjects through personal emotion and a spiritual apprehension of reality, his goals in publishing *Dread* went far beyond the personal.

The poems in this collection explore a far wider range of emotion and experience than those in his previous collection, *Earth*. They range from celebrations of the joys and sorrows of Partisan life ("Moon with a Halo," "The Game," "After the Meeting," "Dialectics") to meditations on the meaning of the struggle against Fascism ("Rain," "Moonlight") to love poems ("Unknown Woman," "The Bay") to musings on morality, death, and immortality ("Hands," "The Stick," "Night Ritual," "Crucifix in a Field"). Through all of them, particularly the Partisan poems, runs the thread of what one critic, writing about Kocbek's war diaries, called Kocbek's "activist engagement with history," conducted "without ideological or political bias, but from the point of view of a constructive and . . . religiously dedicated and responsible person. He juxtaposes the world of cruel political and military pragmatism with original existential questions. . . . Kocbek-the-believer is always juxtaposed with Kocbek-the-heretic."

Kocbek's conflict between faith and skepticism found frequent expression in these poems in the form of paradox—his quintessential trope. In "The Game" the speechmaker "stammers in his dreams," a lowly peasant "commands the brigade," and "the quiet woodcutter is full of questions." He develops this idea further and with great playfulness in "Dialectics."

> *The builder demolishes houses,*
> *the doctor advances death*
> *and the fire brigade chief*
> *is the arsonists' secret leader,*
> *clever dialectics says so*
> *and the Bible says something similar:*
> *he who is highest shall be lowest,*
> *and he who is last shall be first.*

In another fine poem, "Hands," Kocbek endows the concept with a metaphysical dimension that ends in a confession. The poet describes himself as living "between my two hands / as between two brigands, / neither knew/ what the other did. / The left hand was foolish because of its heart, / the right hand was clever because of its skill." In a military skirmish he is forced to turn and flee, experi-

ences a stark fear of death, and falls among thorns that draw blood
from those same hands.

> *I spread them like the cruciform branches*
> *of the great temple candlestick,*
> *bearing witness with equal ardor.*
> *Faith and unfaith burned with a single flame,*
> *ascending hotly on high.*

Dread established Kocbek's reputation as the best poet then writing
in Slovenian (indeed one of Slovenia's best poets ever), and also as the
"father" of Slovenian modernism, which was being rediscovered and
built upon by the younger generation. In 1967 he published *Document*,
a second volume of his wartime diaries, to universal acclaim, and this
was followed by the republication of the first volume, *Charter*, and in
1969 *Report*, a third selection of his poetry. It emerged that before *Re-
port*, Kocbek had completed another selection of poems, *Pentagram*,
devoted mainly to his Partisan years, that he had withheld out of po-
litical prudence, and this appeared for the first time in a two-volume
edition of *Collected Poems* in 1977, together with two new and hith-
erto unknown selections, *Embers*, and *Bride in Black*.

The *Collected Poems* of 1977 consolidated Kocbek's reputation
and filled in some of the gaps in his earlier work. Of particular
interest are the early poems in *Pentagram*, which demonstrate
Kocbek's talent for personalizing the political and politicizing the
personal. The word "pentagram" refers in part to the five-pointed
star of the Partisans during World War II, and of the Yugoslav Com-
munist Party then and thereafter (a much subtler emblem than the
Soviet hammer and sickle), but also, and more powerfully, to an an-
cient cabbalistic sign that was traditionally popular in Slovenia as a
talisman against demons (it was carved on the cribs of the newborn
for good luck). This rich double meaning naturally attracted
Kocbek's attention, and in a title poem of the same name he sug-
gests a continuity between ancient resistance to evil and the war-
time crusade against a new kind of demon.

> *History rambles through nature,*
> *man is mysteriously hawk-eyed.*

Day is a spearman's bright aura,
night a shield armed with a star,
a tribe's talisman in bloody glory.

From the clay come the words of wise shamans:
the stubborn and promising light of this star
will deliver us from evil,
will hand us the keys to ultimate joy,
will reconcile power with freedom.

But the demons that Kocbek most feared were within. The Pentagram cycle contains two separate poems with the same title, "Guilt," both of them dealing with his own ambivalence in the face of violence in war. In one he writes:

Obedient to the pitiless command,
I cannot quell the seething in my breast.
What can I do with this exorbitant "I"
That is turning me into a beast?

This recalls an earlier comment in his essay on Kierkegaard: "action is will, after action comes guilt." During the Partisan campaigns, action was inevitable, of course, and couldn't help but bring out the "beast" in him. But there was another and larger beast, the beast of war, that engendered fresh waves of guilt and doubt, as in "On Fire."

I am riding the beast,
To be or not to be,
Anxieties increase,
I cannot leave.

Even more powerful is his wonderful poem, "The Stick," in which Kocbek compares the piece of wood he holds in his hands to a shepherd's crook, a walking stick, an officer's cane, a conductor's baton, a divining rod, or a magician's wand, and imagines all the positive uses he can make of it. But he will do none of these things for they are "risky and foolish." Instead

I will break it over my knee
and throw it down a deep ravine,

so that its heavy notches
may measure my fall.

In keeping with this habit of interiorizing his conflicts, Kocbek wrote very few poems that might be called overtly political, and even when he did they were wrapped in allegory. In "Parrots," for example, he imagines a plague of parrots.

Green and yellow, they screeched
in our houses, kitchens and gardens;
unclean, ravenous, and vulgar,
they invaded our bathrooms and bedrooms
and finally settled in people.

It is not hard to see these parrots as political watchdogs, but Kocbek also compares them to the demons that actually enter people and possess them, as in the bible, and the solution he envisages is equally internal and psychological. The parrots will be driven out and will die once the wise men in the community realize what is happening, assume the necessary responsibility, and ultimately take action.

Kocbek similarly takes responsibility for his own actions while remaining defiant and welcoming the consequences.

When I spoke
they said I was dumb,
when I wrote
they said I was blind,
when I walked away
they said I was lame.
And when they called me back
they found I was deaf.
They confounded my senses
and judged I was mad.
Now I am glad.

This selection of Kocbek's poems covers many other dimensions of his work and his world. One such is the patriotic strain that emerges in poems like "Black Sea," with its wry political barb aimed at Serbia and Russia, and in his wonderful long poem, "Lippizaners," on the white stallions that perform in Vienna's world-renowned Imperial Riding Academy, but are bred and raised on the limestone pastures of western Slovenia.

> *Others have worshiped holy cows and sacred dragons,*
> *thousand-year-old turtles and winged lions,*
> *unicorns, double-headed eagles, phoenixes,*
> *but we have chosen the most beautiful animal,*
> *it has proved itself in battle and in circuses,*
> *carried princesses and golden monstrances,*
> *and that is why the Viennese emperors spoke*
> *French with clever diplomats,*
> *Italian with pretty actresses,*
> *Spanish with almighty God,*
> *German with unschooled stable boys,*
> *and with their horses, Slovene.*

During the last few years of his life Kocbek enjoyed the fame that was his due. He was lionized in literary circles in Slovenia, and was permitted to travel, at last—to England, France, Germany, Austria, Italy—to read his poems and meet other writers, becoming especially friendly with the German Nobel Prize–winning novelist, Heinrich Böll. But he was never recognized by the political establishment, and in 1974 Böll was forced to mount an international campaign on his behalf when, in an interview for his seventieth birthday, Kocbek boldly mentioned the mass murder of monarchist "White" prisoners by the "Red" Communists after the war and became the subject of an orchestrated hate campaign. By now, however, he was far too prominent to be sanctioned or jailed. His work was being translated and read throughout Europe, and he was recognized, as one critic put it, as one of the five thinkers and intellectuals in Slovenian history who had shaped the nation. Six years later, after his death in 1981, he was granted a state funeral.

Although Kocbek's status as a dissident (albeit one who never went to jail) had something to do with his fame in the last two decades of his life, his true stature derives from his power as an artist. He was miraculously able to rise, indeed almost float, above the topical concerns of the moment, even when they pressed upon him with the greatest urgency and unpleasantness. From the earliest poems in *Earth* through to his last, unfinished poem with its typically defiant title, "I haven't done playing with words" (which ends this selection), Kocbek engaged life with an openness to experience, an attentiveness to its hidden messages, an indefatigable playfulness, and a mastery of the lyric form that were the unmistakable marks of a major talent.

As for his personal credo, it was best summed up in a 1974 essay that he wrote titled "On Poetry, Freedom and Necessity."

> *As a writer I am completely independent, no force on earth can tell me what to do. . . . Spiritual revelations apart, poetry has been the most important thing in my life, a refuge for my inventions and fantasies. It was able to protect me, anticipate events, point the way ahead, and confirm my actions at moments of gravest doubt or indecision. It gave me the power of protest, rebellion, and revolutionary action in the contradictory world of today."*

From EARTH

NA MOJIH RAMAH ŽDIJO NEME PTICE

Na mojih ramah ždijo neme ptice
in ves dan gleda v moje bledo lice
nekoč pozabljena skrivnost.

Menih stoletni gledam v čarni svet,
kako v večerni zemlji rahlo sled
zapušča moj skrivnostni gost.

Čuj, ves dan slišim svetih psalmov spev,
presunjeň slišim radosten odmev
otožno žejne žalosti.

Ah, ves dan vame tihe žene zro;
po ves dan jemljem žalostno slovo
od lepih zemeljskih oči.

Zdaj sem na sredi dneva tih in sam.
Zdaj grem in vem, odkod, zakaj in kam:
ljubezen večno grem iskat.

V daljavi nočni čaka tihi hram,
le tebi svoje mlado srce dam,
odprite krila večnih vrat.

SILENT BIRDS PERCH ON MY SHOULDERS

Silent birds perch on my shoulders
all day my pale face is scanned
by a once forgotten mystery.

An ancient monk, I observe the enchanting world,
what a tender trace is left on the evening earth
by my mysterious visitor.

Listen! All day I hear the sounds of sacred hymns,
I thrill to the joyful ring
of sadly ardent affliction.

Yes, all day the quiet women study me,
all day I take my sorrowful leave
of beautiful earthly eyes.

Now I am calm and alone in the midst of the day,
now I will go, knowing whence, where and why;
seeking a love that endures.

In the distant night a silent temple awaits,
to thee alone I pledge my youthful heart,
open wide those eternal gates.

SONCE JE PREPREŽENO S PAJČEVINO

Sonce je prepreženo s pajčevino,
zrak je domač kakor v zastrti
kmetiški sobi in v gozdno trohnobo
se je s hriba zakotalil težek sad.
Zdaj zdaj zaškriplje samokolnica
ali se zasliši šumot dolgih koruznih
listov in motna pesem poznih čebel
nad ajdo.

Mi pa, prijatelji, vrzimo torbo
čez rame in pojdimo v gorice, da čujemo
klopotec in napolnimo majoliko.
Sleherni si mora odgrniti meglo izpred
oči in poškropiti s starim vinom zoreče
trte ter pogledati izpred hrama v dolino,
kjer se naše mlade žene v somraku
bosih stopinj bojijo.

The sun is wreathed in cobwebs,
the air is homely, as in a curtained
cottage parlor, and a heavy fruit
has rolled downhill into the rotting wood.
Now and then a wheelbarrow squeaks,
there is a sudden rustle in the long leaves
of corn, and the lazy hum of late bees
over the buckwheat.

And we, friends, will toss our knapsacks
onto our shoulders and go to the vineyards to hear
the bird scarers and fill our jugs.
We must brush the mist from
our lids and sprinkle the ripening vines
with old wine, then look down from the pressing shed
into the valley, where our young women go in fear
of bare footsteps in the dark.

MOČNA RDEČA JUNCA GRESTA

Močna rdeča junca gresta počasi
po cesti, kakor da ne vesta, da vlečeta
breme. Kola se pregibljejo s počasnimi
sunki, veriga visi pred levim zadnjim
potačem in se maje brezglasno in
v enakih zamahih, kakor bi ne hotela
motiti soglasja. Juncema kapa skozi
nagobčnik peneča se slina in pušča
tanko mokro sled z okroglimi vozli.
Rdeče blesteča se koža jima toplo diši,
in ko s sanjajočim voznikom stopata
v gozd, se zdi, da izginjata za večno.

Čez nekaj časa vidim rdeča junca,
kako kimata iz gozda po hribu navzgor.
Nič se nista spremenila, v tej mirni
zemlji ni časnosti.

A PAIR OF STRONG YOUNG OXEN GOES SLOWLY

A pair of strong young oxen goes slowly
along the road as if unaware they are
hauling a load. The cart moves with measured
jerks, a chain by the left rear
wheel swings silently in equal
arcs as if unwilling
to spoil the harmony. Foaming saliva
drips from the oxen's muzzles leaving a thin
wet trail of circular blobs.
Their glistening russet hides smell warm,
and as they enter the wood with their dreamy
driver, it seems they are disappearing forever.

A little later I see the young red oxen
nodding out of the wood and up the hill.
They haven't changed a bit. In this peaceful
land time has stopped.

ŽENE GREDO Z DELA

Žene gredo z dela in se med njivami
vzpenjajo v hrib. V praznem večeru se
pomikajo kakor čreda živali in širijo
nosnice. Ko se bližajo gozdu, hipoma
zapojo zategnjeno pesem kakor fantje,
in ko na koncu njihov zavlačujoči
glas močno zategne in na mah utihne,
se zdi, da slišimo na trati njihove bose
stopinje kakor zamolklo osamelost.

Po vseh jesenskih vratéh gredo žene
z dela, njihovo petje odmeva po šumah
in grenko prst bi si metal v usta od žalosti,
ko jih slišim.

The women are coming from work and
climb the sloped fields. Like a herd of
animals, they move through the empty evening, flaring
their nostrils. As they near the wood, they break
like young boys into a high-pitched song,
and when their keening voices end
in a powerful sob, and fall abruptly
silent, it's as though we can hear their bare
footsteps in hollow loneliness on the turf.

Through all the autumn meadows the women
are coming from work, their song echoes in the
woods, and I could stuff my mouth with bitter soil
in sorrow over their sound.

TEŽKO DEBLO STISKA ZADNJI KOŠ GROZDJA

Težko deblo stiska zadnji koš grozdja,
tisti, ki so se razveseljevali, so odšli, le dva
moška glasova še govorita modro in enakomerno
v globoko noč. Dobrota nočne besede se meša
v tišino, vonj mošta omamno seda
na ilovnata tla in staro deblo
od časa do časa zaškriplje.

Potem tudi moža utihneta, prvi sede
na prazne vreče in omamljen od negibnosti
zaspi, drugi pa osamljen prisede in se mu
v spanju pridruži. Zunaj migljajo zvezde,
potem dogori luč, kapljanje utihne, nato
dolgo ni ničesar, dokler se iz doline jutranji zvon
ne oglasi.

The heavy bole presses the last basket of grapes,
those who were celebrating have left, just two
men's voices talk steadily and wisely far into the night.
The goodness of nocturnal words melts
into the silence, the smell of must settles dizzyingly
onto the clay floor, and now and again the old bole creaks.

The men grow quiet too. The first, sitting
on empty sacks, is stunned by the stillness
and falls asleep. The other, now lonely, moves closer
and joins him in sleep. Stars twinkle outside,
then the lamp burns low, the dripping stops, and
for a long time there is nothing, until, down in the valley,
the morning bell tolls.

O ŠUM VODÀ IN SESEDANJE VESOLJA

O šum vodà in sesedanje vesolja,
žena, položi uho na mojo stran, tam
odzadaj traja večna slovesnost, drži me
za roko, ne morem ti povedati, kako
gromka je veličastnost, objemi me tesnó,
moje telo razganja svetla smrt, oči
mi ne vidijo več, ušesa ne slišijo več,
srce mi lije na nočno travo, potegujoči
veter me trga, sladko razpadam,
zemlja še ni dokončana. O strašni
Sin živega Boga, nemo te kličem, pomagaj
mi v moji ljubezni.

O noise of waters, collapse of the universe,
woman, put your ear to my side,
yonder stretches eternal solemnity, hold my
hand, I cannot tell you how
thunderous is this magnificence, clasp me tight,
bright death is bursting my body, my eyes
see no more, my ears hear no more,
my heart spills onto the nocturnal grass,
the heaving wind tears at me, I fall sweetly apart,
the earth is not finished yet. O terrible
Son of the living God, I mutely implore you, help
me in my love.

GLASNO VAS POZDRAVLJAM, TOVARIŠI ŽIVI

Glasno vas pozdravljam, tovariši živi,
težaki, pisarji, pustolovci in potapljači,
vseh morij ribiči in vseh zemelj poljedelci,
vojščaki, gobavci, roparji in žene vseh.

Vetrovi prinašajo glasove,
iz hriba na hrib se prižigajo bakle,
prapori plapolajo, v silnem taboru vrvimo,
čutimo enako kakor živali pod večer.

Zemlja bobni pod prihajajočimi, ljudstva
se zbirajo za veliki dan. Veseleč se zbora
ležimo drug ob drugem, urejajoči se in bučni
čakamo sredi noči na trombe glas.

Loud greetings to you, my living comrades,
laborers, scribblers, adventurers, and deep-sea divers,
fishers of all the seas and farmers of all the lands,
warriors, lepers, bandits, and all your wives.

The breezes are bringing familiar voices,
beacons are blazing from hill to hill,
flags are aflutter, we seethe in our mighty camp,
feeling like animals when night falls.

The earth rumbles at their approach, the peoples
are gathering for the great day. Gladdened by this assembly
we lie side by side, settling ourselves, boisterously
waiting in the night for the trumpet to sound.

Pijan od spreminjanja ležim na tleh
in čelo ob zemljo pritiskam. Tresem se in se
ne upam dvigniti, preveč vidim in preveč
slišim, vsa zemlja se vrti, brezgibni zamahi
in neslišni utripi nas razganjajo, vedno
nova omama prihaja od guganja in nas ustavlja.

Potem se dvignemo in zopet stečemo naprej,
za teboj, ki se nikdar ne ustaviš, in zopet
se utrujeno opotekamo in spet se vržemo
za teboj, o neutrudnost človeška, zadnja
ljubezen prestrašenega srca. Nič usmiljenja
ne prosimo, le trdno se moramo držati,
tovariši, in ne smemo se izpustiti.

Drunk with change I lie on the ground
and press my brow to the earth. I tremble and
dare not rise, I see too much, I hear
too much, the whole earth spins, this motionless swinging
and soundless throbbing is driving us apart, the rocking induces
ever more stupor and checks us.

Then we rise and run forward again,
after you who never stop, and again
we stagger wearily and again rush
after you, O human persistence, last
love of a frightened heart. We ask
no quarter; comrades, we must just hold
fast and never let go.

❧ ZEMLJA, IZ TEBE SE DOTIKAM VSEGA

Zemlja, iz tebe se dotikam vsega, zemlja,
vate se vračam, moje meso diši po sveti
daritvi in smrtni žalosti, dolgo bom
gledal navzgor, ponoči in podnevi.

Zemlja, naš grob, kako si lepa, zemlja,
sladko temno zrno med zrni, od tvoje
globine sem zmeden, ptiči čivkajo nad nami
eden med njimi nas bo pozobal.

EARTH, I GET EVERYTHING FROM YOU

Earth, I get everything from you, earth
to you I return, my flesh smells of holy
sacrifice and mortal sorrow, long will I
look upward by day and by night.

Earth, our grave, how lovely you are, earth,
I am a sweet dark grain among grains, bewildered
by your depths, birds chirrup over our heads,
one of them will peck us up.

❧ *From* DREAD

DEŽ

Zamolkli boben bobna,
dež pada v dolgo, dolgo noč,
zamolkli boben bobna,
usoda trka oberoč,
zamolkli boben bobna,
okoli mene je obroč,
zamolkli boben bobna,
v obupu vpijem na pomoč,
zamolkli boben bobna,
ne morem več od tebe proč,
zamolkli boben bobna,
spominjam se trepetajoč,
zamolkli boben bobna,
tako je že bilo nekoč,
zamolkli boben bobna,
dež pada v dolgo, dolgo noč.

RAIN

The hollow drum drums
rain falls the whole night long
the hollow drum drums
fate knuckles its old song
the hollow drum drums
I am closed in a ring
the hollow drum drums
I cry for help in my pain
the hollow drum drums
I cannot leave you again
the hollow drum drums
shivering I recall
the hollow drum drums
it happened once before
the hollow drum drums
rain falls the whole night long.

Med svojima rokama sem živel
kakor med dvema razbojnikoma,
nobena izmed njiju ni vedela,
kaj je počenjala druga,
levica je bila nora od srca,
desnica pa pametna od spretnosti,
ena je jemala, druga izgubljala,
druga pred drugo sta se skrivali
in opravljali polovična dela.

Ko sem danes bežal pred smrtjo
in padal in vstajal in padal
in se plazil po trnju in skalovju,
sta mi bili roki enako krvavi.
Razpel sem ju kot žrtvena ročaja
velikega tempeljskega svečnika,
ki z enako vnemo pričujeta.
Vera in nevera sta bili en sam plamen,
vzdigoval se je visok in vroč.

HANDS

I have lived between my two hands
as between two brigands,
neither knew
what the other did.
The left hand was foolish because of its heart,
the right hand was clever because of its skill,
one took, the other lost,
they hid from one another
and left everything half-finished.

Today as I ran from death
and fell and rose and fell
and crawled among thorns and rocks
both were bloody.
I spread them like the cruciform branches
of the great temple candlestick,
bearing witness with equal ardor.
Faith and unfaith burned with a single flame,
ascending hotly on high.

MESEČINA

Vso noč se opotekam
po globoki mesečini,
na levi in desni ležijo
zeleno gola trupla
kakor marmorni kipi,
potegnjeni iz morja,
ki jih je nekoč zalilo
v stebrastih svetiščih
in jim je sidro odtrgalo
glavo ali desnico z vencem.

Zdaj vem, potapljač sem,
spustili so me v globočino
brezumne zgodovine,
težka voda me zaustavlja,
alge me zapletajo,
potopljeni svet miglja
od nagnjenih stvari sveta,
žrtve ležijo po areni,
porušeno nebo še vedno
pada v svoj sarkofag.

Vso noč se opotekam
po globoki mesečini,
na levi in desni ležijo
zeleno gola trupla,
zmeda neznanskega reda
me preliva in spreminja,
šele nocoj sem zvedel
za neizrekljivo resnico,
kruteje bom živel
in nežneje umrl.

❧ MOONLIGHT

All night I stumble
through deep moonlight,
to the left and right of me
lie greenishly naked bodies,
like marble statues
pulled from the sea
that once drowned them
in columned temples,
and an anchor has severed
a head or a hand with a wreath.

Now I know I am a diver,
I have been lowered into the depths
of foolish history,
dense water resists me,
seaweed plucks at me,
the sunken world glimmers
with the world's things askew,
victims lie around the arena,
the ruined sky falls and falls
into its sarcophagus.

All night I stumble
through deep moonlight,
greenishly naked bodies
lie to left and right of me,
the chaos of a colossal order
engulfs and changes me,
only tonight have I learned
the unutterable truth,
I shall live more cruelly,
And more tenderly die.

MESEC S KOLOBARJEM

Ob meni so ubili človeka.
Imel je mater, ki ga je rodila,
in očeta, ki mu je delal igrače,
imel je brate in šegavega strica
in deklico s plavimi kitami,
imel je voziček in konjiča
in skrinjo s pisanimi sanjami
in potok, kjer je lovil ribe.

Približal se mi je s hitro hojo
in me ves zasopel dohitel,
ustavila sva se kot znanca,
v rokah drži kletko s ptiči
in brašno za dolgo pot,
v žepu ima pismo za čez tri doline,
med usti pa ubrane orglice,
zdaj zdaj se bodo oglasile.

Tišina polni nebeške prostore,
veter pojema v košatih lipah,
jabolka dišijo s stare police
in kruh se obrača proti vratom,
že se je vtihotapil vame.
Začel sem se poslavljati od sveta,
v temnem oknu nesrečnega srca
je zažarel mesec s kolobarjem.

MOON WITH A HALO

The man beside me was killed.
He had a mother who bore him
and a father who made him toys,
he had a brother and a playful uncle
and a little girl with blond braids,
he had a wooden cart and a wooden horse,
a trunkful of colored dreams
and a brook where he used to fish.

He had approached at a brisk walk
and was short of breath when he reached me,
we'd halted as if we knew one another,
he held a cage with birds in his hands
and victuals for a long journey,
there was a letter in his pocket for three valleys away,
a sweet-tongued mouth organ between his lips
was ready to burst into song.

Silence fills the heavenly spaces,
the wind dies in the branching lindens,
there is a smell of apples from the old shelf
and the bread turns toward the door,
he has tiptoed into me already.
I have begun to take leave of this world:
suddenly, into the unhappy heart's dark window
shines a moon with a halo.

RAZPELO NA POLJU

Kadar so za telovo postavili
oltar podenj, so nekateri videli,
kako je počasi odprl oči
in razširil ozke nosnice,
blažen od kadila.

Potem so si sledile dišave,
vonji žita in trav, megle,
dim požarov, duh po smodniku;
skrivnostni strel mu je šel
skozi čelo in mu še bolj nagnil
glavo s trni in s senenimi bilkami,
izgubil je človeško podobo
in postal strašilo.

Vse se je razdivjalo
in zakoprnelo po strašnem.
Zdaj visi le še na enem žeblju,
in ko bo neke noči veter
od neznanskega čaščenja poskočil,
se bo iznenada odtrgal,
stopil na varno zemljo
in jo poljubil.

When they placed the altar beneath him
on Corpus Christi, some saw
how he opened his eyes
and his narrow nostrils flared,
intoxicated by the incense.

Then came other odors,
the scent of wheat and grasses and mist,
smoke and the smell of gunpowder;
a mysterious shot pierced his brow
and bent his head still lower
with its thorns and wisps of hay,
he lost his human form
and became a scarecrow.

The world ran amok
and lusted for horrors.
Now he hangs by a single nail,
and one night when the wind
rises in furious adoration
he will tear himself away,
step down onto the safe earth
and kiss it.

IGRA

Škrbasto posodo držim v rokah
in v vrsti čakam pred kotlom.
In ko pogledam predse in nazaj,
me presune čudežno spoznanje,
šele zdaj se vidimo v pravi luči.
Nekdo nas je spremenil in razodel,
kakor da bi premešal karte,
poredno, izzivalno in neznansko,
predvsem pa tako kot v vsaki igri,
da so naključja skrivnostno pravilna,
vsakomur je priklical skrito resnico.

Kdor je ril pod zemljo, hodi po nebu,
in kdor je govoril na trgu, jeclja v sanjah,
kdor je spal na senu, poveljuje brigadi,
in kdor je tiho drvaril, kar naprej sprašuje,
kdor je znal Homerja, gradi bunkerje,
in kdor je jedel v Parizu, si rezlja žlico,
pivec liže roso, pevec posluša tišine,
ministrant nastavlja mine, skopuh zbira rane,
hlapec je zvezdogled, strahopetec bombaš,
pesnik mulovodec in sanjač telegrafist,
zapeljevavec deklet pa je varen vodič.

Škrbasto posodo držim v rokah
in gledam predse in gledam nazaj
in se ne morem nagledati podob,
procesija prikazni, romanje duhov,
migljanje resnic, razodevanje usod.
Nekdo nas je spremenil in določil,
kakor da bi premešal karte,
poredno, izzivalno in neznansko.
Potem pa se ozrem še po sebi
in se zagugam od sanjske teže,
vsi so v meni kakor v mladi materi.

I hold a chipped bowl in my hands
and wait in the camp kitchen line.
And when I glance forward and back
I am struck by a marvelous insight:
only now do we see ourselves properly.
Someone has changed and exposed us,
as though shuffling a pack of cards,
wantonly, provocatively, strangely;
but above all, as in all games,
the odds are mysteriously even
and he has reminded us of our secret truth.

He who burrowed now walks upon air,
the declaimer of speeches now stammers in his dreams,
he who slept upon straw now commands a brigade
and the quiet woodcutter is full of questions;
he who quoted Homer is building bunkers
and he who dined in Paris is shaping a spoon;
the drinker licks dew, the singer harkens to the silence,
the sexton sows mines, the miser collects wounds,
the farmhand is a stargazer, the coward a commando,
the poet is a mule driver, the dreamer a telegraphist,
and the local Casanova is a trusted guide.

I hold a chipped bowl in my hands
and I look to my front and look back,
and I can't take in all the images,
ghosts in procession, spirits on a pilgrimage,
truths glimpsed and fates revealed.
Someone has changed and defined us,
as though shuffling a pack of cards,
wantonly, provocatively, strangely.
And then I turn and look at myself
and reel under the weight of dreams—
they are all inside me, as in a young mother.

PO MITINGU

Pravkar sem govoril ljudem,
zbranim okoli zelenega odra,
med starimi drevesi in njih sencami
sem se premikal na norih hoduljah,
vihtel sem roke in kričal v veter
in se nagibal nad neme postave
in si z nasilnimi sunki utiral pot
skozi tesne zenice v skrivnostno srce.

V eni uri sem napravil glasno pot,
ki jo v tišini hodijo stoletja,
podvizal sem se v pošastno deželo
in zasopljen pulil korake iz mulja,
vedno bolj sem hitel in govoričil,
vedno bolj sem se vrtel, nesrečni čarodej,
nazadnje sem odpiral usta kot riba na suhem
in se naglušen vdal strašni premoči.

In zdaj, ko so se ljudje šumno razšli
in je na poteptani trati ostal le veter
in poševno sonce sije na potrgane vence,
sem nesrečen kakor po prazni ljubezni.
Slišim nežni porog in razpadam od nasilja,
zmeden sem od svojih lastnih besed,
čutim domotožje po eni sami,
po eni sami in neizrekljivi.

Večer zahaja čist in brezdanji,
moje besede pa letajo brez gnezda,
kmalu bodo poginile žejne in lačne.
Vzdignil se bom v noč in potrkal na vrata
in klical ljudi in jih vabil nazaj:
Vrnite se, otroci človeški, in mi odgovorite!
Usedel se bom med vas in vas poslušal
in do čistega jutra mi bo odleglo.

I have just finished speaking to the people
gathered round my green platform;
among ancient trees and their shadows
I moved on mad stilts,
I waved my arms and yelled into the wind
and loomed over their silent figures,
and by violent pushing cleared a path
through narrowed eyes to their mysterious hearts.

In one hour I shouted a path
that the centuries walk in silence,
I hastened to a spectral country,
and panting, wrenched my steps from the mire;
I hurried and babbled more and more;
more and more I spun, a luckless wizard;
at the end I gasped like a fish out of water
and yielded, half-deafened, to a terrible force.

And now when the people have departed, murmuring,
and only wind remains in the trampled clearing,
and the slanting sun shines on tattered garlands,
I am sad, as after failing to make love.
I hear a gentle mocking and collapse from the force of it,
I am puzzled by my own words,
and yearn for one only,
one only that is unutterable.

Evening descends, pure and bottomless,
and my words fly without a nest,
soon they will die of hunger and thirst.
I will rise in the night and knock on doors
and call the people and invite them back:
Come back, sons of men, and answer me!
I shall sit among you and listen to you,
and by the pure morning I will have found relief.

NEZNANKA

Nepozabljivi čudež v rajskem vrtu,
spreminjasta podoba Lepe Vide,
nerazvozlana pravljica v sanskrtu,
na sanjskem jadru veter Atlantide.

Po ulicah sveta hitiš, omama
menjav, ekstaz in čarov palimpsest,
neznanskokrat neznana lepa dama
začenjaš v meni žalostno povest.

Zdaj—angelskih peruti sladka tenja,
prečistega ljubimca večna slava,
zdaj—prazna groza grešnega želenja,
z razkošno slo odrešena skušnjava.

Ti—ranjena divjina na Diani,
jaz—pravljičnega princa zlati meč,
zato si sneg na moji vroči dlani,
ki pade tiho in ga že ni več.

UNKNOWN WOMAN

Momentous miracle in the garden of paradise,
mercurial effigy of Vida the Fair,
indecipherable fairytale in old Sanskrit,
dreaming sails in the wind of Atlantis.

Opiate of change and ecstasies, palimpsest
of charms, hastening through the streets of the world,
thousand times unrecognized beautiful woman,
you evoke a sorrowful fable in me.

Now the sweet silhouettes of angels' wings,
eternal glory of the immaculate beloved,
now the empty horror of sinful desire,
temptation redeemed by a sumptuous craving.

You are the wounded wilderness on Diana,
I the gold sword of a fairytale prince,
you are the snowflake upon my hot fingers
that quietly falls and is gone forever.

ZALIV

S tihimi vesli sem obstal
nad blaženo globočino,
nikoli nisem videl nazaj
do samega začetka sveta
kakor v tisti mesečini.

Spominski zaliv je bil
sredi neodkritih otokov,
čoln iz školjk sem pripel
med predpotopne ribe,
nerojeni so me gledali.

Napravila sva si šotor
iz otroških zmajev,
ležišče iz tigrovih šap,
temó iz ugaslih kresov
in lino iz ranljivosti.

Ko sem jo položil v ris,
med čudež in protičudež,
je začela prerokovati,
v blaženosti se je spomnila
svojega večnega imena.

Ljubezen se ji je omračila
od darežljivih prikazni,
izbralo si jo je nasilje
neizrekljive svetosti,
počasne in nežne.

Tedaj sem izumil sebe
in mnogoterost dlani
in izrekel sem besede,
ki jih poslej nihče več
ne bo mogel ponoviti.

With silent oars I paused
over blissful deeps,
never had I seen back
to the beginning of the world
as I did in that moonlight.

It was memory's bay
among undiscovered islands,
I tied up my boat of shells
amidst antediluvian fishes,
still unborn, looking at me.

The two of us made a tent
from children's kites
and a bed of tigers' paws,
we made darkness from extinct bonfires
and a peephole out of vulnerability.

When I laid her down in the magic circle
between miracle and antimiracle
she began to prophesy,
in her ecstasy she remembered
her eternal name.

Her love was darkened
by generous phantoms,
she was chosen by violence
of unutterable holiness,
gradual and tender.

Then I invented myself
and the multiformity of my palm,
and I spake words
that nobody will ever
be able to repeat.

NOČNI OBRED

Hiša se je nagnila pod krošnje,
veter je pokleknil pred vrata,
strah si je podvil rep,
zvezde so se razvrstile,
angeli so čaščenju
izpostavili noč.

Zemlja je kadilnica,
temà žerjavica,
in človek kadilo.
Padam na ogenj,
na sladko tlenje,
postajam dišava.

NIGHT RITUAL

The house leaned beneath the treetop,
the wind knelt at the door,
fear put its tail between its legs,
the stars arranged themselves in order,
angels exposed the night
to worship.

Earth is the censer,
darkness the ember
and man the incense.
I fall on the charcoal,
on the sweet cinders
I become the scent.

PONOČNI VETER

Ko se mu je opolnoči
topli veter za vogalom
nenadoma postavil po robu
in ga ni pustil dalje,
mu je spominsko zaigralo,
torej ste se vrnili, prekleti,
in pri priči je vedel,
vrnila se je njegova ura.

Veter je igrivo poskočil,
zakadil se je vanj in ga podrl,
sovražnik je najboljši prijatelj,
prebudi te iz nevarnega ždenja,
polepša ti zlato na spominu,
kajti nobena bitka na zemlji
ni nikoli do kraja dobljena,
začnimo, kjer smo nehali.

Bila je obljubljena noč
s sanjami pod strašnim gradom,
človek mora uničiti pošast,
babica je prva govorila o njej,
ukleta kraljična je vabila,
padali smo v kri in se vzdigovali,
rušili okope, tekali po hodnikih
in se brezumno zapletali v sanje.

Skočil je v prebujeni veter,
zaletel se je v strmo steno
in predrl prekleto črto,
potem pa ostal v brezvetrju,
sovražnika ni bilo več,
veter je sovražnik, ki mine,
zmaga je ukleta kraljična,
bitka ni nikoli dobljena.

One midnight, when a warm wind
round the corner
brought him up short,
stopping him from going on,
he had a flash of memory—
so you've come back, damn you,
and at once he knew
his hour had returned.

The wind sprang playfully,
leaped at him and knocked him down,
the enemy is your best friend,
he rouses you from dangerous apathy,
burnishes the gold on your memory,
for no battle on earth
is ever won to the finish,
let's start where we left off.

It was the promised night
of dreams under the terrible castle,
man must destroy the monster,
grandma was the first to mention it,
the enchanted princess issued her summons,
we fell, bloodied, and rose again,
destroyed the trenches, rushed through the corridors
and got senselessly entangled in dreams.

He sprang at the aroused wind,
crashed into the steep wall,
broke through the infernal line,
and was caught in a sudden lull,
the enemy wasn't there any more,
the wind is an enemy that passes,
victory is an enchanted princess,
the battle is never won.

Gradbenik podira hiše,
zdravnik približuje smrt
in poveljnik požarne brambe
je skriti vodja požigalcev,
pravi bistra dialektika
in sveto pismo pravi podobno:
kdor je zgoraj, bo spodaj,
in kdor bo poslednji, bo prvi.

Pri sosedu leži nabita puška,
pod posteljo se skriva mikrofon
in hčerka je obveščevalka.
Soseda pa zadene kap,
mikrofonu odpove elektrika
in hčerka hodi k spovedi.
Vsakdo se obesi koštrunu na trebuh,
ko se tihotapi iz Polifemove votline.

Iz cirkuškega šotora slišim
razglašeno nočno glasbo,
mesečniki hodijo po visoki vrvi
in krilijo z negotovimi rokami,
pod njimi pa vpijejo prijatelji,
da bi jih do kraja prebudili,
kajti kdor je zgoraj, mora doli,
in kdor spi, naj zaspi še trdneje.

The builder demolishes houses,
the doctor advances death
and the fire brigade chief
is the arsonists' secret leader,
clever dialectics says so
and the Bible says something similar:
he who is highest shall be lowest,
and he who is last shall be first.

There's a loaded rifle at the neighbor's,
a microphone under the bed,
and the daughter is an informer.
The neighbor goes down with a stroke,
the microphone's current fails,
and the daughter goes to confession.
Everyone clings to a ram's belly
when sneaking from the Cyclops' cave.

In the night I hear clashing music
from the circus tent,
sleepwalkers walk the highwire,
swaying with fluttering arms,
while their friends yell underneath
to rouse them from sleep,
for whoever is up must come down,
and whoever sleeps, let him sleep more soundly.

● ČRNO MORJE

Vse naše vode
težijo vate,
Črno morje.
Rosa juter
in večerne nevihte
in vsi vrelci
žuborijo vate,
tatarsko morje.
Vsi snegovi in plazovi
in vse povodnji
hitijo vate,
turško morje.
In z njimi se trga
naša dobra prst
in s svetim pepelom vred
pada na tvoje dno,
bizantinsko morje.
In z našo prstjo
se usedajo vate
naša telesa,
neusmiljeno morje.
V tvojih algah smo že
in v tvojih požrešnih ribah,
del tvoje globine smo že,
Črno morje.

BLACK SEA

All our waters
rush to thee
Black Sea.
Morning dew
evening showers
and all our streams
gurgle into thee
Tartar sea.
Our snows and avalanches
and all our floods
race down to thee
Turkish sea.
And with them our good soil
is washed away
to fall with the sacred dust
onto thy bottom
Byzantine sea.
And with our earth
our bodies too
settle into thee
merciless sea.
Now we are in thy weeds
and in thy ravenous fish,
Now we are stuck in thy depths,
Black Sea.

PALICA

Kaj naj storim s svojo palico,
ko me je začela prehitevati?
Ali naj jo vržem v pastirski ogenj
ali jo podarim šepavcu na cesti
ali oglednikom v obljubljeno deželo?
Ali naj jo vzdignem v zrak,
da z njo pomirim ljudski hrup,
ali jo podstavim svojemu bratu,
da si bo v temi zlomil nogo?
Ali naj jo vržem na morje,
da bo rešila utapljača,
ali jo zasadim v polje,
da bo za strašilo v vetru?
Ali naj jo obesim v romarsko cerkev,
da bo pomnožila svetinje,
ali pa jo pokopljem v gozdu,
da je ne najdejo biriči?
Ali naj jo dam nevednemu očetu,
da si bo z njo ukrotil sina,
ali pa jo izpostavim rosi,
da mi bo znova zazelenela?
Ali naj jo izročim vodji zbora,
da mu bo uredila glasove,
ali jo dam zanosnemu dečku,
da mu bo podprla šotor?
Ali naj z njo odkrijem studenec,
da bo napojil puščavo,
ali pa z njo pričaram kruh
iz klobuka na čarovnem odru?

Nič vsega tega ne bom storil,
kajti vse to je drzno in noro,
prelomil jo bom na kolenu
in jo vrgel v globoko brezno,
da bodo njeni glasni rovaši
izmerili moj pad.

What shall I do with my stick
now that it has begun to outdistance me?
Shall I throw it on a shepherd's fire,
or give it to the lame man on the road,
or to scouts reconnoitring the promised land?
Or shall I raise it in the air
to still the people's tumult,
or use it to trip my brother
so he breaks his leg in the dark?
Or shall I throw it into the sea
to save a drowning man,
or plant it in a field
to stand like a scarecrow in the wind?
Or shall I hang it in a pilgrim church
to increase the number of relics,
or bury it in a wood
where the bailiffs can't find it?
Or shall I give it to an ignorant father
so he can use it to tame his son,
or leave it out in the dew
so it turns green again?
Or shall I hand it to a choirmaster
to harmonize voices,
or give it to an eager boy
to use it to prop up his tent?
Or shall I divine a spring with it
to water the desert,
or use it to conjure bread
from a stage magician's hat?

No, I will do nothing of the sort,
for those things are risky and foolish:
I will break it over my knee
and throw it down a deep ravine,
so that its heavy notches
may measure my fall.

MILOST

Ko se je nocoj nebo
nenadoma pordečilo
in se zatem poglobilo
v svetlobo brez imena,
sem vztrepetal.
Iz brezdanje rane
je začela teči
tiha kri
in me zalila.
Nežno nasilje
me je obšlo,
začel sem razpadati
kakor lipovina
v junijskem večeru.
Oddivjal sem na goro
in si odpel tesnobo,
približala se mi je
skrivno kakor blaznost.
Vse je bilo presveto.
In nikjer ni bilo
niti ene temne misli,
ki bi me skrila,
niti enega greha,
ki bi me pomiril,
niti enega izdajstva,
ki bi me rešilo.

GRACE

When the sky suddenly
reddened tonight
and deepened
to a nameless light
I trembled.
Silent blood
flowed
from that bottomless wound
and flooded me.
I was overwhelmed
by a gentle violence,
I began to fall apart
like a lime wood
on a June evening.
I stormed to the mountain
and unbuttoned my anguish,
it approached me
stealthily like a madness.
Everything was utterly holy.
Nowhere was there
one dark thought
to hide me,
not one sin
to soothe me,
not one betrayal
to save me.

POKRAJINA

Duh divjih živali
se bliža hišam,
nosnim ženam
se premikajo ustnice,
zreli prostor diši
po mastni snovi
in zamolklem žitu.
Sadovi so nahranili črve,
rože so se vrnile
v nočni čebelnjak,
pokrajina je legla
izza svoje podobe.
Tišina starinsko rožlja,
spomin vzdiguje sidro,
mesečina se igra
s pavovim repom.
Stvari postajajo večje
od svoje navzočnosti,
pijanci se ne napijejo žeje,
živali ne pridejo do dna
svoji nedolžnosti,
veter se hrani od prepadov
in temà od tatov.
Svet je preluknjan
z domotožnimi bolečinami,
vrtim se v risu
kakor v poročnih sanjah,
ne morem se spomniti
rešilnega obrazca.

LANDSCAPE

The scent of wild animals
nears the houses,
the lips of pregnant women
move,
ripe space smells
of oily stuff
and darkened corn.
Fruit feeds the worms,
roses return
to the nocturnal beehive,
the landscape reclines
behind its image.
Silence rattles anciently,
memory weighs anchor,
moonlight plays
with a peacock's tail.
Things grow bigger
from their presence,
drunkards can't drink enough thirst,
animals can't reach the bottom
of their innocence,
the wind feeds on precipices
and darkness on thieves.
The world is riddled
with homesick pains,
I turn in a charmed circle
as in wedding dreams,
I cannot recall
a formula to set me free.

SELITEV

Konji na paši
skačejo vso noč
čez mesečinske prepade.
Ženske poslušajo
škrtanje v pohištvu,
otroci padajo
v spanju iz postelj,
moški se prebujajo
z glavami ob nožišču.
Nočni veter
vzdržuje pijance
v poševnem čudenju,
ko srečujejo prikazni.
Trpeča svetloba
prebuja rajnke
in polni z njimi
božje poti.
Svetniki nagibajo glave
na starih podobah,
vrata se odpirajo
sama od sebe,
začenjamo se seliti.

MIGRATION

All night the horses
in the meadow jump
over moonlit ravines.
Women listen
to scratching in the furniture,
sleeping children
fall from their cots,
men wake
with heads at the foot of the bed.
The night wind
props up drunkards
in tottering astonishment
as they bump into ghosts.
Long-suffering light
wakens the dead
and funnels them
into pilgrimages.
The saints in old pictures
incline their heads,
doors open
by themselves,
our migration is under way.

Otrok igra na orglice,
igra nežno in sanjavo,
nebo se je zagugalo,
strehe so se upognile,
vrata so se odprla,
stopnice so poskočile,
drevesa so začela hoditi,
vse bi rado odšlo v Tibet.

Pazite na predmete,
ko jih jemljete v roke
ali jih mečete na smetišče.
Utrujeni mož gre zvečer domov,
na rami nese svetlo sekiro.
Ni izgubljenih predmetov
in ni najdenih predmetov,
poznamo le spremenjene stvari.

Knjiga odide v glavo,
žebelj se zarije v križ,
klobuk postane strašilo
in lampijon zagori
v neznanskem otrokovem spominu.
V svoje vnebovzetje bodo stvari
odnesle več človeškosti
od nas, ubogih ljudi.

A child plays a harmonica,
sweetly and dreamily,
the sky is set a-rocking,
the roofs are a-bobbing,
the door swings wide open,
the stairs leap up,
trees start walking,
all would like to go to Tibet.

Be careful with things
when you pick them up
or throw them on the trash heap.
The weary man walks home at night,
his bright axe over his shoulder.
There are no lost things
and no found things either,
we know only of things that have changed.

A book sinks into the head,
a nail is buried in the cross,
a hat turns into a scarecrow
and an oil lamp flares
in the boundless memory of a child.
On their assumption into heaven
things will take more of humanity with them
than we poor men.

POZIV

Spomnimo se,
kako smo teptali zemljo,
krotili zveri,
podpirali nebo
in kričali drug drugemu
slovesna povelja,
da smo vzdržali v votlini,
ki jo je sonce izdolblo
v vesoljno temó.

Spomnimo se,
kako smo votlino
razširili s hrbti,
da je svet zastokal,
višine zaplahutale,
globine zaškrtale,
strani neba zavpile
in himen skrivnosti
zakrvavel.

In zdaj se spomnimo
še velikih prerokb,
rojeni smo za čudeže,
hodili bomo po morju,
letali po zraku,
se žogali z zemljo
in jo izgubili v temi,
potem pa si poiskali
vsak svojo zvezdo.

❧ *SUMMONS*

Let us remember
how we tramped the earth,
tamed beasts,
propped up the sky,
shouted to one another
solemn commands,
to hold out in the cave
quarried by the sun
from cosmic darkness.

Let us remember
how we widened that cave
with our shoulders
so that the world groaned,
the heights quivered,
the depths rasped,
the sky screamed,
and the hymen of the mystery
began to bleed.

And now let us remember
the great prophecies too,
we were born for miracles,
we shall walk on the sea,
we shall fly through the air,
we shall play ball with the earth
and lose it in the dark,
then each of us will seek
his own star.

DOBRA SLUTNJA

Odšel sem navzgor
po pobočju dneva,
kakor da bi iskal
stavbišče za katedralo.
In ko sem prišel
na samotno jaso,
sem se ustavil,
bila je tiha
kakor srečno gnezdo
ptička kraljička.
Zaprl sem oči,
nagnil glavo
in zašepetal:
Res je, prijateljica,
prav tu bi mogel ležati,
dve pedi globoko,
izmirjen in spremenjen
kakor zaliv v večeru
ali zlato na ikoni.
Prav tu pri tebi
bi mogel zaspati,
snoval bi roso in sonce,
hranil travo in veter,
nosil ljubezen prepelic
in smukanje zajcev.
Prav tu bi se lahko
do kraja izmiril,
presvetljeni sanjač,
indijanski deček,
pod pahljačo zarij,
v obredih sonca
in na trepalnicah teme.
Žarel bi s kresnicami,
gugal bi se z zvezdami,
hlipal s tajnimi ljubimci
in se vračal nazaj
v ognjeno deželo.

PRESENTIMENT

I set off to climb
the slope of the day
as if seeking
a site for a cathedral.
And when I came
to a lonely clearing
I stopped.
It was quiet
like the happy nest
of a jenny wren.
I closed my eyes,
bent my head
and whispered:
it's true, my dear,
I could lie right here
two spans deep,
at peace, transformed,
like a bay at twilight
or the gold on an icon.
Right here with you
I could fall asleep,
I could devise the dew and the sun,
feed the grass and the wind,
carry the love of quails
and the scurrying of hares.
Here I could easily be
wholly reconciled,
an enlightened dreamer,
a Red Indian boy
beneath the fan of the sunsets
in the rituals of the sun
and on the lashes of the dark.
I could glow with the glowworms,
swing with the stars,
sob with secret lovers
and return once more
to the fiery land.

❧ MOLITEV

Sem,
ker sem bil,
in vsakdo
me bo mogel
pozabiti.

In vendar
moram reči:
sem
in bil sem
in bom,
in zato sem več
od pozabljanja,
neizmerno več
od zanikanja,
neskončno več
od niča.

Vse je večno,
kar nastane,
rojstvo je močnejše
od smrti,
vztrajnejše
od obupa in samote,
silnejše
od hrupa in greha,
slovesnejše
od zavrženosti.
Nikoli
ne bom prenehal biti.
Nikoli.
Amen.

PRAYER

I am
because I was,
and everyone
will be able
to forget me.

And though I must say
that I am
and I was
and I shall be,
I am more
than oblivion,
immensely more
than negation,
immeasurably more
than nothing.

All that exists
is eternal,
birth is stronger
than death,
more persistent
than despair and loneliness,
mightier
than clamor and sin,
more solemn
than desolation.
Never
shall I cease to be.
Never.
Amen.

From PENTAGRAM

NA NOČNI STRAŽI

Noč roma od postaje do postaje,
v temi si dopolnjuje svojo pot.
Stojim na mestu in drvim skoz kraje
in čase in ne vem, ne kam ne kod.
In vsakikrat me plašni srh prešine,
ko slišim žabe, pse in peteline.

Nekoč sem varen legal v mlado spanje,
in v sanjah spajal srčnost in preplah.
V temini me je čaralo regljanje,
da sem pozabljal na prvinski strah.
Zdaj pa se vrača kot spominska groza
in strašna noč postaja gluha loza.

Pesjad se zdaj od žalostnega kraja
zglasi ter srce in duha stesni.
Kot nepotešena ljubezen laja,
kar sem neznanskega spočel v temi,
in zvesta tožba psov odpira rane,
vse globlje in skrivnostno znane.

Nazadnje se tesnobna noč na dvoje
razkolje in razkrije strašni red,
petelin tretjič budnico zapoje
in že je svet v nešteto zank ujet.
Nevarna luč razpada v srebrnike,
tema prešteva kupljene jetnike.

Kaj naj stori uboga moja duša?
Srebro slepi oko, lovi uho,
resnici služiti s preklici skuša,
v korist si spremeniti grešno zlo.
Noč roma od postaje do postaje
in skriva svet zvestobe in izdaje.

Night roams from station to station,
completing itself in the dark.
I stand still and rush through places
and times, and I don't know where to turn.
And I experience a thrill of shy terror
when I hear a frog, a dog, or a rooster.

I used to lie safely in youthful slumber,
in dreams I fused daring and fright,
in the gloom I was charmed by the croaking
and forgot my primitive dread.
But now it returns like a remembered horror
and the ghastly night is hollow and dead.

A pack of dogs bays from that melancholy region,
stunning my spirit and heart,
that colossal thing I begot in the darkness
emits a howl like unrequited love,
and the faithful dirge of the dogs then opens
wounds that are deeper and secretly known.

The anguished night splits asunder at last,
and reveals a terrible order,
a cock crows its triple alarum
and innumerable loops snare the world.
The dangerous light dissolves into ducats,
the darkness counts its purchased slaves.

What will my poor soul do in the future?
Silver dazzles me, haunts my ear,
tries to serve the truth by recantation
and make use of iniquitous evil.
The night roams from station to station
hiding a world of treason and faith.

DVOJNOST

Kakor da bi nenadoma stopil
iz šuma v tišino,
se je pred menoj odprla
omamna ravnina z mirnim dihom,
plemenita ženska kraljevske lepote,
davno udomačena zemlja,
ognjišča, vrtovi in grobovi.

Zaprl sem oči
na meji dveh svetov,
sanjskega in resničnega,
srečnega in nesrečnega
in zašepetal:
O Antigona,
ko se bom vrnil z lova,
bom pokleknil predte
in ti služil!

Zlomljeni glasovi so mi odgovorili
z ravnine:
podvojeni udarci perice na vodi,
podvojen konjski peket,
podvojen pasji lajež,
podvojen otroški krik,
podvojeno zvonenje.
Stisnilo me je:
vse je zlomljeno,
svet se je razklal
na dvoje
in se ne more več združiti.
Sadovi sveta so dozoreli,
prišla je temna ura.
Veter se je nenadoma vzdignil,
mi razmršil lase,
potem pa planil v globino,
moral sem se naglo oprijeti
žilavega debla.

DOUBLED

It was as if I had suddenly stepped
from noise into silence,
before me stretched
a stupendous plain, peacefully breathing,
a noble woman of royal beauty,
earth tamed from ancient times,
hearths, gardens and graves.

I closed my eyes
at the junction of two worlds,
the dreamed and the real,
happy and unhappy,
and whispered:
O Antigone,
when I return from the hunt
I will kneel before you
and serve you!

Broken voices answered me
from the plain:
the doubled slapping of the washerwomen,
the doubled thunder of horses' hooves,
the doubled barking of the dogs,
the doubled crying of the children,
the doubled tolling of the bells.
I was stunned:
everything was broken,
the world had been split
into two
and could not be pieced together again.
The world's fruit had ripened,
the dark hour had come.
Suddenly the wind rose,
ruffled my hair,
and hurtled into the depths.
I was forced to cling tight
to a sinewy tree.

KAKO BOM OBSTAL

Najprej si mi bila mlada mati
naučila si me sladkega tipanja,
oprijemal sem se zemlje in sanj,
obešal se na mehki trebuh živali
in se plazil po mladi travi,
preprijemal sem razne slasti,
varovala si me v igri in hrabrila.

Potem si me začela mučiti z bliski
in gromi, plašila si me s cigani,
slačila si mi telo in dušo,
podstavljala mi nogo in vrtoglavice,
slepila si me, me varala z dišavami,
majala mi stebre svetišč, zmedla si
mojo čistost in mi podarila žejo.

In ko si zblaznela od starosti,
si mi postala sovražna in zvita,
vrgla si me v mojo črno kri,
da se zdaj plazim po zemlji in snegu
čez trnje, pogorišča in grobove,
tipam te in otipam samo tebe golo,
brezumno, nesrečno in nesramno.

Kako bom obstal, ko se vrne dan
in bodo vrabci znova noro začivkali?
Kako bom obstal, ko si bomo podajali
zvezde iz roke v roko in bom stopal
čez prag nedolžnih? Kako bom obstal
sredi pepelnega obreda in se mi bo
tišina približala kakor jalova ženska?

❧ HOW SHALL I BE?

First you were a young mother to me,
you taught me the sweetness of touching,
I clung to earth and dreams,
hung from the soft bellies of animals
and crawled through the young grass,
I sampled a variety of delights,
you protected my play and encouraged me.

Then you tormented me with thunder
and lightning, frightened me with gypsies,
stripped me body and soul,
tripped me and made me dizzy,
blinded me, deceived me with smells,
rocked the columns of temples, confounded
my purity and gave me the gift of thirst.

And when you went mad from old age,
you turned cunning and hostile toward me,
you thrust me into my black blood
so that now I crawl over earth and snow,
through thorns and graves and burnt-out homes,
I fumble for you and find you naked,
unhinged, unhappy and unashamed.

How shall I be when day returns
and the sparrows chirp madly again?
How shall I be when the stars are passed
from hand to hand and I cross
the threshold of the innocent? How shall I be
in that ashy ritual when silence approaches
me like a barren woman?

Naša zemlja, dragocena skrinja,
nosi rdeče vrezan pentagram.
Glejte, to je magična svetinja!
Da bi zlo zatrl in rešil hram,
zarotilec bese z njo zaklinja.

Iz davnine hranimo orožje,
z enim potegljajem rogljast ris.
Nepretrgano peterorožje
more uročiti smrtni ugriz,
ko v človeku zalezuje božje.

Zgodovina tava po naravi,
človek je s skrivnostjo jasnovid.
Dan je ostri kopjanik v svetlavi,
noč je z zvezdo oborožen ščit,
znamenje rodu v krvavi slavi.

Modri žreci govore iz ila:
hkrati uporna in koledna luč
nas bo zvezda zlega ubranila,
izročila nam do sreče ključ,
silo in svobodo uskladila.

Naša zemlja, dragocena skrinja,
nosi rdeče vrezan pentagram.
To je naša magična svetinja,
z njo nam slehernik rešuje hram,
kadar bese z zvezdami zaklinja.

Our land is a precious coffer,
bearing a carved red pentagram.
Look, with its magic totem
the wizard banishes demons,
crushes evil and saves the temple.

For eons we have borne weapons,
drawn a horned ring at one stroke.
That uninterrupted pentacle
magically heals the fatal bite
that ambushes man's divinity.

History rambles through nature,
man is mysteriously hawk-eyed.
Day is a spearman's bright aura,
night a shield armed with a star,
a tribe's talisman in bloody glory.

From the clay come the words of wise shamans:
the stubborn and promising light of this star
will deliver us from evil,
will hand us the keys to ultimate joy,
will reconcile power with freedom.

Our land is a precious coffer,
bearing a carved red pentagram.
This sign is our magic totem,
which everyman will use to save our temple
when he bewitches the demons with stars.

❧ VOTLINA

Ogenj je ugasnil,
veter se je ustavil,
človek je utihnil
in se obrnil nazaj,
odprla se je noč,
zemlja je ladja
v čudežni kraj.

Ležim na hrbtu
in gledam v mesec,
srebrna divjad hiti
čez rdeči mlaj
in me lovi,
zdaj je želva, zdaj srna,
zdaj pravljični zmaj.

In tedaj se v votlini
neznanske tišine
srečam s samim seboj,
prav tu sem bil
in ne vem, kdaj,
in prav to sem bil
in ne vem, kaj.

THE CAVE

The fire has died,
the wind has dropped,
the man has gone quiet
and turned away,
night has opened,
the earth is a ship
to wonderland.

I lie on my back
and look at the moon,
silver beasts speed
across the red blot
and chase after me,
now it's a tortoise, now a deer,
and now a magic kite.

Then, in a cave
of immense silence,
I meet myself,
It's true I was here
and I don't know when,
and I was also the same
but I don't know how.

V DREVESNI SKORJI LIK

In ko se tretji dan zgrozim v tišini,
pod sivim nebom v blodno luč ujet
in se zgubim v brezdanji bolečini
kot sužénj z daljnim upanjem prevzet,
me v hipu prešumi zelena slava
in sname z mojih čutov pajčolan,
da sem v igrivem soncu nova stava
in v junijski daljavi velikan.

In spet se vrnem v obnovljeno stvarstvo
kot v pravljično resnico zvesti škrat,
da brž ko prej dosežem divje varstvo
prvin, nevarnih sanj in norih nad.
In glej, tedaj, se mi stori enako,
v drevesno skorjo urežem srca lik,
v desetih letih se bo zvilo v spako,
odkrilo moj pošastni spomenik.

And when I shrink in silence on the third day,
caught beneath a gray sky in erratic light,
and lose my way in bottomless grief
like a slave possessed by a distant hope,
I am momentarily seized by a green glory,
my senses are stripped of their thin veil,
I am a new wager in the playful sunlight,
in the June vista a mighty giant.

And again I step into a new universe
like a faithful goblin into fabled truth,
in a trice I gain the wild protection
of the elements, rash dreams and mad hopes.
And lo, sweet thoughts start to steal upon me
and I carve a heart in the bark of a tree.
Ten years will twist it to an ugly scowl,
a monstrous monument—myself revealed.

NOČ OROŽJE SNEMA

Mesec sence riše,
človek diha tiše,
sapa krošnje giblje,
pokoj srca ziblje,
nežno nam se drema,
noč orožje snema.

Tu je dobro biti,
varno smo zakriti,
v čistem dnu temine,
kjer bede prvine,
ogenj že pojema,
noč orožje snema.

Vse smo dnevu dali,
trudni smo postali,
človek v spanje zajde,
da se v sanjah znajde,
usta so že nema,
noč orožje snema.

Tihi klici sove
mirijo duhove,
vse se vsemu bliža,
nekdo me prekriža,
duh telo objame,
noč orožje sname.

NIGHT DOFFS ITS WEAPONS

The moon etches shadows,
the man's breath slows,
a breeze stirs the trees,
our hearts rock in peace,
we are gently dozing,
night doffs its weapons.

It is good to be here,
safe in our lair,
in the pure pit of the dark,
where the elements stand guard,
the campfire's in embers,
night doffs its weapons.

We've given our all to the day,
and now we are drained,
a man strays into sleep,
to explore his dreams,
mouths are now wordless,
night doffs its weapons.

The soft hooting of owls
calms our poor souls,
all things draw nigh,
someone blesses me,
soul embraces body,
night doffs its weapons.

❧ *From* REPORT

Termiti so napadli pokrajino,
izvotlili mostove in spomenike,
mize in postelje so razpadle v prah.
Bacili so se zalezli v laboratorije,
naselili so se na čistih instrumentih
in mimogrede ukanili učene može.
Vse se je zgodilo pošastno tiho.

Pri nas so se zaredile papige,
zelene in rumene so zavreščale
po vrtovih, hišah in kuhinjah,
požrešne, nesnažne in prostaške
so vdrle v kopalnice in spalnice
in se nazadnje naselile v ljudeh.
Vse se je zgodilo pošastno glasno.

Nihče med nami ne zna več lagati
in nihče ne more povedati resnice,
govorimo jezik neznanega plemena,
kričimo, kolnemo, zavijamo, tulimo,
širimo usta in napenjamo oči,
še dvorni norec je zblaznel
in vrešči kakor vsi drugi.

Nekje pa stojijo možje v krogu
in nemo gledajo v mirno središče,
nepremično stojijo in blaženo molčijo,
ramena so jim vedno širša
pod starim bremenom tišine.
Ko se bodo nanagloma obrnili,
bodo papige v nas poginile.

❧ PARROTS

Termites attacked the province,
undermined bridges and statues,
turned beds and tables to dust.
Germs invaded laboratories,
settled on sterilized instruments,
fooling wise men in the process.
It all happened so horribly quietly.

In our case it was a plague of parrots.
Green and yellow, they screeched
in our houses, kitchens, and gardens;
unclean, ravenous, and vulgar,
they invaded our bathrooms and bedrooms
and finally settled in people.
It all happened so horribly loudly.

No one knows how to lie any more
and no one can tell the truth;
we speak the tongue of an unknown tribe,
we yell and curse and howl and wail,
open our mouths and pop our eyes;
even the court jester has gone insane
and screeches like everyone else.

Somewhere men stand in a circle
gazing mutely toward the still center;
they stand motionless in blessed quiet,
their shoulders growing ever broader
beneath their ancient burden of silence.
When they suddenly turn to face outward
the parrots in us will die.

❧ TIHOTAPSTVO

Ljudje se branijo kakor vedo in znajo.
Oponašajo igro otrok v mraku,
gredo se skrivalnice, odlagajo
svojo odvečnost in se vprašujejo,
čemu sem noga, odkod sem dobil roko,
beseda kazalec mi je sumljiva,
sploh želim, da bi svet razpadel,
in tako dalje, potem pa zazehajo
in si s ščetko umijejo zobe
in zaspijo s palcem v ustih,
higiensko izpraševanje vesti.

Človek je pristaš aseptične vere,
zavest je le klinični proces,
vse drugo je ostalo zapuščeno
in se skrivaj lepi na prste,
leze za nohte in med sramne kodre,
nabira se v očeh in v ušesnem bobniču,
počasi se vzpenja na hrbet,
v spanju drsi v sanje,
se tihotapi v kri in srce
ter se maščevalno zarije
v levi palec desnega stopala.

CONTRABAND

People defend themselves as best they may and can.
They imitate children's games in the dark,
play hide and seek, postpone
their redundancy and ask themselves,
why a leg, where did I get my arm,
the term index finger sounds suspicious to me,
I really wish the world would collapse
and so on, and then they yawn
and brush their teeth
and fall asleep with thumbs in their mouths,
a hygienic interrogation of conscience.

Man clings to an aseptic creed,
consciousness is a clinical process,
all the rest has been abandoned
but sticks surreptitiously to your fingers,
creeps behind the nails or into your pubic hair,
collects in your eyes and eardrums,
slowly climbs up your back,
slips into your dreams while you are asleep,
smuggles its way into your blood and heart
and vengefully buries itself
in the left toe of your right foot.

Kar se osebne varnosti tiče,
ti svetujem pametno vajo:
zdaj pa zdaj se nenadoma in scela
obrni v tujo stran sveta
s tistim trenom očesa,
ki smo z njim nekoč odkrivali
mesečino na sončni uri,
nevidne stopinje po stropu
in polnoč tujega cesarstva,
kajti v našem gradu straši
razodeta domišljija divjega moža.
Zato ti svetujem preprosto vajo,
kadar moreš, se zazri sunkovito
v poljubno stran in se ne preplaši,
resnično je le to, kar je nenadno,
zatrto, neprijetno in nerazložljivo.
Nocoj boš morda ulovil sledeči
neobvezni, toda poučni program:
škorpijon bo lezel čez ženino krilo,
v ključavnici se bo obrnil sosed,
zemlja bo zahajala na zaslonu,
fotelj bo nastopil pot na Japonsko,
na postelji ti bo vzcvetel žafran,
v kaminu bodo zagorele ledene gore,
otroci bodo zazidali okna,
na pajčevini bo zabingljala blagajna,
v žarnici se bo zrušil matematični sistem,
ura bo odbila dvanajsto čez pol tretjo,
na zidu pa boš bral mene tekel ufarsin.

❧ EXERCISE

With regard to your personal safety
let me recommend this sensible exercise:
now and then try quickly turning
toward the unknown side of the world,
in that wink of an eye
with which we once discovered
moonlight on a sundial,
invisible footprints on the ceiling
and the midnight of a foreign empire,
because our castle is haunted
by a wild man's exposed fantasy.
That's why I advise a most simple exercise.
Whenever you can, stare abruptly
in any direction, and don't be afraid,
for only what is sudden,
suppressed, unpleasant, and inexplicable is real.
Tonight you might catch the following
instructive but not obligatory program:
a scorpion crawling up your wife's skirt,
your neighbor turning in the keyhole,
the earth setting on a screen,
your armchair starting off for Japan,
saffron blooming on your bed,
icebergs catching fire in your hearth,
children walling up the windows,
a cashbox dangling from a cobweb,
the mathematical system collapsing in a lightbulb,
the clock striking twelve past half past two
and on the wall the words *mene tekel ufarsin.**

---

*These Hebrew words appear in the Book of Daniel, verse 25. Their meaning is given variously as follows: "God hath numbered thy kingdom and finished it." "Thou art weighed in the balance, and art found wanting." "Thy kingdom is divided and given to the Medes and Persians."

DEKLIŠKI PREDPASNIK

Ko se je na vrhu griča ustavila
in se obrnila v moj topli veter,
je od strahu spustila predpasnik,
bil je poln starih hiš in drevja,
zakotalilo se je po pobočju
in se uredilo v neizrekljivo vas,
stopil sem v najbližji hram
in predrl zid neznanskega spomina,
vonji in dišave so me opijanili,
čarovnija me je premagala
in me za polovico večnosti omračila,
prebudil sem se zelo pozno
in se naslonil na veter,
bil je še vedno topel,
počasi sem ji napolnil predpasnik,
hiše, dvorišča, plotove, hleve,
seno in mesečino, vzdihe in smeh,
zvonik sem ji položil vanj previdno,
da ne bi preveč zacingljalo.

GIRL'S APRON

When she stopped at the top of the hill
and turned into my warm wind
she dropped her apron in fright,
it was filled with old houses and trees,
they all rolled down the slope
and formed an indescribable village,
I stepped into the nearest wine cellar
and pierced the wall of huge memory,
I got drunk on odors and aromas,
overpowered by a magic
that unhinged me for half eternity.
I woke very late
and leaned on the wind,
which was still warm,
slowly I filled her apron
with houses, yards, fences, and stables,
with moonlight and hay, sighs and laughter,
and took extra care with the belfry,
to make sure it didn't tinkle too much.

KLIMAKS

Noč širi lečo
in vzame vase
zemljo z zvezdami
in z njimi povzdigne
tebe in mene v ognjeno nebo,
že sva zubelj v mogočni bakladi.

Ko pa odpreš
svoje globoke oči,
si še močnejša od noči,
obsežeš prostor in čas,
igro divjajočega vesolja,
ekstaze, katastrofe, zakone,
vseh sedem eonov stvarjenja.

Tedaj prebudiš mene,
da razširim svoji zrkli,
nagnem se nad tvojo igro
in začnem piti večnost tvojih oči,
vso noč premagujem strašno končnost,
dokler ne obvladam tvoje ljubezni
in ne postanem gigant med giganti,
samotni moški.

❧ CLIMAX

Night dilates its lens
sucks in
the earth and stars
thrusts them and
you and me into the flaming sky
like a torch in a fiery procession.

And when you open
your bottomless eyes
you are still mightier than the night,
you encompass both space and time,
the dance of the savage cosmos,
ecstasies, catastrophes and laws,
and the seven eons of creation.

Then you wake me,
I widen my pupils,
I crouch over your dance
and drink the eternity of your eyes,
all night I subdue my terrible limitations
until I have mastered your love
and become a giant among giants,
a solitary man.

❧ MELODIJA

Mesec na hribu, hriba ni,
veter v globeli, globeli ni,
na ribniku čoln, čolna ni.

Ti si ob meni, tebe ni,
vzdigujem roko, roke ni,
veter mi oči slepi.

Bila si jaz, bil sem ti,
niti tebe niti mene več ni,
ničesar ni, nikogar ni.

❧ DITTY

Moon on the hill, no hill,
wind in the dell, no dell,
sail on the pond, no sail.

You beside me, you're gone,
I raise my hand, hand gone,
my eyes are blinded by the wind.

Once I was you and you me,
no more you and no me,
nothing and nobody.

❧ ZDAJ

Kadar sem govoril,
so rekli, da sem nem,
kadar sem pisal,
so rekli, da sem slep,
ko pa sem odšel od njih,
so rekli, da sem hrom.
In ko so me klicali nazaj,
so ugotovili, da sem gluh.
Vse čute so mi zmešali
in presodili, da sem blazen.
Zdaj sem srečen.

❧ *NOW*

When I spoke
they said I was dumb,
when I wrote
they said I was blind,
when I walked away
they said I was lame.
And when they called me back
they found I was deaf.
They confounded my senses
and judged I was mad.
Now I am glad.

❧ PONT

Tu, kjer sem, je Pont.
Pont je izgnanstvo.
Izgnanstvo spominja na raj,
toda raja se ne morem spomniti,
sovražnikova sila je ugasnila,
ne izziva me več s strastjo
in ne vrača me več vase.

Hodim po poljih in gorah,
odpiram knjige in gledam ptice
in iščem svoje nasprotje,
kličem ga in koprnim po njem,
da bi me silovito vznemirilo,
toda izgnanstvo je svoboda
brez izzivača in soočenja.

PONTIC

Here where I am is the Pontics.
The Pontics mean exile.
Exile suggests paradise,
but I can't remember paradise,
the enemy's force has faded,
his passion no longer provokes me
nor drives me back into myself.

I walk over the fields and mountains,
leaf through books and look at birds,
and search for my opponent,
I call him and yearn for him
to treat me brutally,
but exile is freedom
with no provocation and no resistance.

● KONEC IGRE

Dolgo časa sem opravljal
dvojniško delo,
ponoči sem bil mlinar,
podnevi dimnikar.
Zvesto sem služil
obema gospodarjema,
poslušal sem šum trajanja
in gledal dim minevanja.
Črni so me imeli za belega,
beli so me videli črnega.
Potem sem slap in dim
potegnil v isto strugo,
isti začetek v isti konec.
Naučil sem se podnevi sanjati
in v spanju opravljati dela.
Tako nisem več razdeljen
na dve tlaki,
ampak spojen v eno bolečino,
pripravljen na vse,
kar prihaja.
Zdaj sem dan in noč hkrati,
voda in ogenj,
moka in pepel.
Ne poznam več tihotapstva
in ne vedežujem več.
Slekel sem se do otroka
in na bregu čakam,
kjer se kiti mečejo v smrt.
Poslušam pradavni glas,
le to si, človek, kar nisi,
in imaš vse,
česar nimaš.

❧ THE GAME IS OVER

For a long time I
did double work,
by night I was a miller,
by day a chimney sweep.
I loyally served
two masters.
I listened to the murmur of duration
and watched the smoke of transition.
Black took me for white,
white saw me as black.
Then I drew the waterfall and smoke
into a single channel,
same beginning and same end.
I learned to dream through the day
and work in my sleep.
Thus I am no longer torn
between two bondages,
I am fused into a single pain,
ready for all
that comes.
Now I am both day and night,
water and fire,
flour and ashes.
I have forsaken smuggling,
I tell fortunes no more.
I have stripped down to a child
and wait on the shore
where whales plunge to their deaths.
I listen to an ancient voice,
O man, thou art only that which
thou art not,
and thou hast everything
thou hast not.

● IGRA NAZAJ

Spomin se mi vozla,
pozaba narašča v vsevednost,
nekdo me bere nazaj.
Ne morem več tajiti,
bil sem zraven, kriv sem,
bil sem v vseh tihotapstvih
in udorih, v vseh nasiljih,
zgodba ni izmišljena,
rešilec me je povozil
in zdaj ne vem, kdo sem.
Dva milijona dvojnikov imam,
eden med njimi je sumljiv,
z žeblji za nohti,
z žerjavico v očeh
in z znano igro v ušesih.
Rozenkranz in Gildenstern
In vsi moji dvojniki,
stopite na oder
in odvijte igro
od njenega konca do začetka,
strah išče svoj spomin,
jaz še vedno nisem jaz,
olje mehanizma deluje tiho
in nimate več veliko časa
za blazna dejanja,
ko pa bodo postavili na odru
četrto steno
in me odvedli,
vedite,
garderoba je na levi.

Memory ties itself in knots,
forgetfulness swells to omniscience,
I begin to speak in a foreign
mother tongue.
I can no longer deny
I was there, I am guilty,
I took part in all that smuggling,
the break-ins, the acts of violence,
it isn't an invented tale,
the ambulance ran me down
and now I don't know who I am.
I have two million doubles,
one of them is suspect
with nails under his fingernails,
embers in his eyes,
and a familiar play in his ears.
Rosencrantz and Guildenstern
and all my doubles
come, step onto the stage
and unspool the play
from its end to its start,
fear seeks its memory,
I am not yet me,
the oiled mechanism works quietly
there isn't much time
for mad deeds,
so when they erect
a fourth wall on stage
and I am taken away, remember,
the dressing room is on the left.

KOPRNENJE PO JEČI

Zamudil sem najvažnejše
duhovne vaje svojega življenja,
ostal sem brez dokaza
o svoji pravi vrednosti,
vsaka ječa je zakladnica,
skrivni predal, ljubosumna
mučilnica, najvažnejša stopnja
krvnikove askeze, preden ga
pohujša gola ženska z nožem v roki,
zamudil sem slast te ljubezni,
kajti laže bi umrl, ko bi
preštel kvadre na tleh samice
in domislil presojne freske
na prašnem steklu ter
se skozi zidove zaziral
v mejne položaje človeštva.
Zdaj si se podrla, celica,
in se razsula v odprtost,
svet ni več odrešna krutost,
zdaj je le še sobotno dvorišče.
Zdaj me ne morete več testirati,
nisem več figura za jaslice,
za lutkarstvo ali nastop robotov.
Pripravljam se za drugačno igro,
glejte, siva miška postajam,
sama majhna skrivališča imam,
nocoj bom prenočil v rokavu otroka
brez desnice, jutri pa bom sanjal
v odmevu sence, ki spi po popotovanju
skozi pravljico brez konca.

I was late for the most important
spiritual exercises of my life,
I am left without proof
of my true value.
Each jail is a treasury,
a secret drawer, a jealous
torture chamber, the most important stage
of an executioner's asceticism before he is
corrupted by a naked woman holding a knife.
I miss the delight of that love,
I would die easier if I had counted out
the squares on the floor of my solitary cell
and in my thoughts completed the transparent frescoes
on the dusty pane,
and gazed through the walls
at the frontier posts of mankind.
Now, my cell, you have collapsed,
disintegrated to openness,
the world is no longer a world of redeeming cruelty,
it's only a sabbath yard.
You can test me no more,
I am no longer a figure for the Christmas crib,
for a puppet show or display of robots.
I am preparing myself for a different game—
look, I am turning into a little gray mouse,
my hiding places are all around,
tonight I shall sleep in the sleeve of a child
with no right hand, tomorrow I shall dream
in the echo of a shadow that sleeps after its voyage
through a fairy tale that has no end.

Nič ti ne pomaga, Pavle,
zate ni nobene krogle,
zate ni nobenega drevesa
in nobenega mlinskega kamna,
obsojen si na življenje,
boj se samega sebe, Pavle.

Nič ti ne pomaga,
gleženj so ti zlomili
in oči napolnili z žerjavico,
jezik so ti zapleli
in te pustili v Diogenovem sodu,
boj se samega sebe, Pavle.

Nič več ti ne pomaga,
zate ni niti črnega konja
niti belega velbloda
niti orla na rdečem nebu,
obsojen si na nesrečno zemljo,
boj se samega sebe, Pavle.

Nikjer ni zidu objokovanja
in velikih kijevskih vrat,
tuji maček pije materino mleko
in prijatelj Hamlet dobiva trebuh,
obsojen si na pošast,
veseli se samega sebe, Pavle.

Nothing can help you, Paul,
there is no bullet for you,
there is no tree for you,
and no millstone,
you are sentenced for life,
fear yourself, Paul.

Nothing can help you,
they have broken your ankle
and filled your eyes with coals,
they have knotted your tongue
and left you in Diogenes' barrel,
fear yourself, Paul.

Nothing can help you now,
for you there is neither a black horse
nor a white camel
nor an eagle in the red sky,
you are sentenced to the unhappy earth,
fear yourself, Paul.

There is no wailing wall for you,
and no great gate of Kiev,
a strange cat is drinking the mother's milk
and friend Hamlet has a paunch now,
you are condemned to be a monster,
admire yourself, Paul.

LIPICANCI

Časnik poroča:
lipicanci so sodelovali
pri zgodovinskem filmu.
Radio razlaga:
milijonar je kupil lipicance,
plemenite živali so bile mirne
ves čas poleta nad Atlantikom.
In učna knjiga uči:
lipicanci so hvaležni jezdni konji,
doma so s Krasa, prožnega kopita,
gizdavega drnca, bistre čudi
in trmaste zvestobe.

In vendar ti dodajam, sinko,
da teh nemirnih živali
ni mogoče spraviti v razvidne obrazce:
dobro je, kadar sije dan,
lipicanci so črna žrebeta,
in dobro je, kadar vlada noč,
lipicanci so bele kobile,
najbolje pa je,
kadar prihaja dan iz noči,
kajti lipicanci so beločrni burkeži,
dvorni šaljivci njenega veličanstva,
slovenske zgodovine.

Drugi so častili svete krave in zmaje,
tisočletne želve in leve s perutmi,
samoroge, dvoglave orle in fenikse,
mi pa smo si izbrali najlepšo žival,
izkazala se je na bojiščih in v cirkusih,
prepeljevala je kraljične in zlato monštranco,
zato so dunajski cesarji govorili
francosko s spretnimi diplomati,
italijansko z zalimi igralkami,

The newspaper writes:
some Lippizaners have taken part
in a historical film.
The radio says:
a millionaire has bought some Lippizaners,
the gentle animals were perfectly quiet
during their flight across the Atlantic.
And a textbook informs us:
Lippizaners are quality saddle horses,
their home is the karst, they are fleet of foot,
with a frolicsome canter, a willing temper
and stubborn loyalties.

But let me add, dear son,
that these restless beasts
cannot be placed in clear categories:
it is good when the day shines,
the Lippizaners are black colts,
it is good when night reigns,
the Lippizaners are white mares,
but it is even better
when day emerges from night,
for the Lippizaners are piebald buffoons,
the court jesters of her majesty,
Slovenian history.

Others have worshiped holy cows and sacred dragons,
thousand-year-old turtles and winged lions,
unicorns, double-headed eagles, phoenixes,
but we have chosen the most beautiful animal,
it has proved itself in battle and in circuses,
carried princesses and golden monstrances,
and that is why the Viennese emperors spoke
French with clever diplomats,
Italian with pretty actresses,

špansko z neskončnim Bogom
in nemško z nešolanimi hlapci,
s konji pa so se pogovarjali slovensko.

Spomni se, otrok, kako skrivnostno
sta spojena narava in zgodovina sveta
in kako različna je vzmet duha
pri slehernem ljudstvu na zemlji.
Dobro veš, da smo zemlja tekem in dirk.
Zato tudi razumeš, zakaj so se beli konji
iz Noetove barke zatekli na naša čista tla,
zakaj so postali naša sveta žival,
zakaj so stopili v legendo zgodovine
in zakaj razburjajo našo prihodnost,
nenehoma nam iščejo obljubljeno deželo
in postajajo zanosno sedlo našega duha.

Kar naprej sem na beločrnem konju,
mili moj sinko,
kakor poglavar beduinov
sem zrasel s svojo živaljo,
vse življenje potujem na njej,
bojujem se na konju in molim na njem,
spim na konju in sanjam na konju
in umrl bom na konju,
vse naše prerokbe sem spoznal
na skrivnostni živali,
in tudi to pesem sem doživel
na njenem drhtečem hrbtu.

Nič temnejšega ni
od jasne govorice
in nič resničnejšega ni od pesmi,
ki je razum ne more zapopasti,
junaki šepajo v svetlem soncu
in modrijani jecljajo v temi,
burkeži pa se spreminjajo v pesnike,
krilati pegazi vedno hitreje dirjajo

Spanish with almighty God,
German with unschooled stable boys,
and with their horses, Slovene.

Remember, my child, how mysterious is the link
in this world between history and nature,
and how differently the spirit springs
in each people on earth.
You know very well we are a land of races and contests,
so you understand why, when they left Noah's ark,
the white horses sought refuge on our clean soil,
why they have become our sacred animal,
why they stepped into the legend of history,
and why they will disturb our future
as they restlessly seek the promised land for us
and become the passionate saddle of our spirit.

I ride my piebald horse on and on,
my dear son.
Like a bedouin chief
I have grown into my animal,
I have traveled on it all my life,
I fight on my horse and I pray on it,
I sleep on my horse and I dream on my horse,
and I will die on my horse,
I learned all our prophecies
on this mysterious animal
and I experienced this poem
on its trembling back.

There is nothing darker
than clear speech,
and there is nothing truer than a poem
that cannot be grasped by reason,
in the bright sunlight, heroes limp,
and in the dark, wise men stammer,
but buffoons turn into poets,
winged pegasuses run faster and faster

nad votlinami naše stare zemlje
in poskakujejo in trkajo,
nestrpne slovenske živali
še vedno budijo kralja Matjaža.

Kdor še ne zna zajezditi konja,
naj se čimprej nauči
ukrotiti iskro žival,
obdržati se svobodno v lahkem sedlu
in uloviti ubrano mero drnca,
predvsem pa vztrajati v slutnji,
kajti naši konji so pridirjali od daleč
in so daleč namenjeni,
motorji radi odpovedo,
sloni preveč pojedo,
naša pot pa je dolga
in peš je predaleč.

over the caves of our old earth,
leaping and banging,
impatient Slovene creatures
still trying to wake King Matthias. *

Whoever can't ride a horse,
must quickly learn
to tame this fiery animal,
to sit easily in the light saddle,
to catch the steady measure of its canter,
and above all to keep his anticipation fresh,
for our horses have run a long, long way
and have far to go,
cars are apt to stall,
elephants eat too much,
our road is long
and it's too far to walk.

*Matthias I (1440–1490), King of Hungary and later of most of the lands that later made up the Austro-Hungarian Empire (including Slovenia), was a legendary monarch who became a folk hero after his death. As one legend begins, he was not really dead, only sleeping in his grave, and would be woken by a fair youth, who would liberate the nation and relieve the sufferings of the poor.

❧ *From* EMBERS

◈ *DREVO*

Zaslišim drevo in ga zagledam,
ležem pod njegovo senco
ali pa ga otipljem in podrem,
razsekam ga in položim v peč
ali sestavim iz njega brunarico,
kar koli storim z njim,
vedno ostane drevo,
nerazdeljivi, neuničljivi
šum vetra podnevi in ponoči,
v peči, na ležišču, v senci,
med vrsticami v časniku
in v dimu med nebom in zemljo,
drevo kot senca in počitek,
drevo kot zibelka in krsta,
drevo kot središče raja,
drevo kot šum in tišina,
drevo kot drevo
in drevo kot beseda.

🌑 *TREE*

I hear a tree and I see it,
I lie down in its shade
or I touch it and topple it,
I chop it into pieces and put it in the stove
or build a cabin with it,
whatever I do with it
it's always a tree,
the indivisible, indestructible
hum of the wind by day and by night,
in the stove, on the bed, in the shade,
between the lines of the newspaper
and in the smoke between earth and sky,
tree as shade and rest,
tree as cradle and coffin,
tree as the center of paradise,
tree as humming and silence,
tree as tree
and tree as word.

❧ KAJ JE Z GORO

Gora še ni bila gora.
Gora še ni gora.
Gora bo skoraj gora.
Gora bo zdaj zdaj gora.
Gora je gora.
Gora je še vedno gora.
Gora je kar naprej gora.
Gora je samo še malo gora.
Gora ni več gora.
Gora ne bo več gora.
Gora ne bo nikoli več gora.
Gora nikoli ni bila gora.
Gora je gora.

The mountain has not yet been a mountain.
The mountain is not yet a mountain.
The mountain will soon be a mountain.
The mountain is almost a mountain.
The mountain is a mountain.
The mountain is still a mountain.
The mountain continues to be a mountain.
The mountain is only just a mountain.
The mountain is no longer a mountain.
The mountain will no more be a mountain.
The mountain will never again be a mountain.
The mountain was never a mountain.
The mountain is a mountain.

NEZNANA LJUBLJENA

Ne poznaš me
in jaz ne poznam tebe,
sinja in zelena barva
se ne trpita,
gosposko vijolična
vleče na sveže rdeče.
Iz starega plemena si,
šepet in kri se ti mešata,
vse na tebi je grenko
in prastaro sladko,
na skrivaj se obiskujeva
in se ljubiva
po zapovedanem redu,
s tresočimi prsti
se pobirava z mize
in se s poljubom
nosiva v drhteča usta.
Včasih spihava prah
z morja, da se raniva čisteje
in v poslednji sapi,
oblečena v kraljevski škrlat,
dišeči lasje so ti peruti,
zato odletiš prva,
jaz pa se spremenim
v zadihanega sla
z izgubljenim sporočilom.

You don't know me
and I don't know you,
azure and green
don't mix,
aristocratic violet
runs to fresh red.
You are from the old tribe,
your whispers and blood mingle,
everything about you is bitter
and immemorially sweet,
we meet in secret
and make love by the usual rules,
with trembling fingers
we help ourselves to one another
from the table
and with kisses
feed our quivering mouths.
Sometimes we blow dust
from the sea to hurt one another more
and with our last breath;
arrayed in royal scarlet,
your fragrant locks are wings,
so you fly away first,
while I change
into a panting messenger
with a lost message.

ČAS PESMI

Pravijo: čas pesmi zahaja,
človek je prodal presežke,
primanjkljaji so utrudljivi,
strah pred smrtjo uničuje
poetiko za poetiko,
kar pišemo, so le znamenja,
samo norec je to, kar ni.

Vsi smo v utrujenem prostoru.
Čas zahaja in zopet vzhaja.
Sleherna tema je čudežna.
Sleherna zmeda je zdravilo.
Sila in nemir se ne ustavita.
Domačija je odšla na tuje
kakor deklica pred zrcalo,
razveselila se je obraza,
morje je neznansko globoko.

Zdaj se vračam, mila moja.
Vrtnarici sije dlan od čarov.
Nikoli ne ponovi kretnje.
Posnemam jo v tetoviranju
vsega živega in izgubljam strah.
Iz sedmih ran svete norosti
puhti omama neverjetne govorice.
Odhajam v podivjane pokrajine.
Vse svoje njive sem dal v prelog.
Matica mi je kar naprej na prahi.
Spoznali me boste po bosih nogah
in po globokih sanjah o gori,
ki je odšla k preroku.

They say the day of the poem is setting,
man has sold the leftovers,
shortages are tiresome,
fear of death destroys
poetics after poetics,
what we write are just signs,
only a fool is what he is not.

We are all in a tired place.
Time sets and rises again.
Each darkness is miraculous.
Every confusion is healing.
Power and unrest never cease.
Home has gone abroad
like a girl before a mirror
delighting in her face,
the sea is immensely deep.

I am returning now, my dear.
The gardener's palm glows with charms.
She never repeats a gesture.
I sketch her by tattooing
everything living and lose my fear.
The seven wounds of sacred madness
reek with the stupefaction of incredible speech.
I depart for rank regions.
I have allowed all my fields to lie fallow.
My queen bee remains wild.
You will know me by my bare feet
and by my deep dreams about the mountain
which has gone to the prophet.

❧ BLAŽENO ISKANJE

Kadar koli se te tiho spomnim, pade z mene vse grešno in tuje,
svet je znova slovesen, nedolžen in sproščen kakor po dobrem
delu. Tedaj zapustim zemljo in stopim z igrivimi stopali na
širno morje. Začnem se potepati zunaj celine, kjer so prodali
lepotico, in jo iščem na gugajočih se tleh. Začnem čarati in
prepevati in vabiti k sebi, igram se z globino navzgor in navzdol,
skačem od vala do vala, po oblakih, skozi prastaro svetovje in
mutasta tla, pojem si pesmi minevanja, poznam vse popevke in
načine glasov, načine ljubezni, načine spominov in prerokb, na
vetru gugam svoje brazgotine, plezam po domišljiji, ves svet je
moj, le pesem dekleta se mi izmika, nekaj pomembnega se mi
oddaljuje, poslušam padanje meščevih krajcev in odmeve
uraganov z Aljaske in šume gozdov v Kanadi, kako se krotko
pasejo in vendar je ne vlovim, čeprav jo slutim talec, potepuh,
čarovnik in ljubimec, iščem dekletovo pesem skozi strašni nič,
blodim kakor najtišja sapa skozi orgelske piščali, kakor trava
skozi lisasto kravo ali kakor utež skozi škripec časa, ves sem že
pokrit s koralami, zato nikomur ne povej, kje sem skrit in kje te
bom našel, ostani vedežna tema in blaženo prizadeta bolečina
pod slapovi čiste reke od mlina do mlina.

Whenever I think quietly of you, all that is sinful and alien falls
away from me, the world is again solemn, innocent and relaxed,
as after work well done. Then I leave the land and my playful
feet step out onto the wide sea. I rove far from the mainland,
where they sold the maiden, and I search for her on the rocking
floor. I conjure, I sing and I coax, I play with the depths, rising
and falling, I leap from wave to wave, from cloud to cloud,
through the primeval cosmos and over the mute floor, I sing
myself songs of transition, I know all the tunes and the ways of
voices, ways of love, ways of memories and prophecies, I rock
my scars in the wind, I clamber through fantasies, the whole
world is mine, only the maiden's song eludes me, something
important recedes before me, I listen to the fall of the moon's
horns and the echoes of hurricanes from Alaska and the hum of
woods in Canada as they tamely graze, and yet still I cannot
catch her, although I sense her, a hostage, vagabond, sorcerer
and lover, I search for the maiden's song through a terrible void,
I wander like the gentlest of zephyrs through organ pipes, like
grass through a spotted cow or like a weight through the pulley
of time, I am already encrusted with coral, so tell nobody where
I am hidden and where I shall find you, remain the knowing
darkness and blessedly stricken pain under the falls of a clear
river from mill to mill.

❧ *From* BRIDE IN BLACK

❧ AMOK

Nobena vojna ne pozna milosti
in noben mir ne pozna trajnosti,
sleherna zmaga je brez veljave
in sleherni mir miruje brez ljubezni.
Najbolj me pomirjajo večerni šotori,
kadar na gasilski veselici zaigra
godba na pihala in po polnoči fantje
začno zateglo prepevati. Tedaj me
sredi mojega šepeta dekletu na uho
obide nekaj divjega in neusmiljenega.
Samemu sebi se hipoma zazdim silen,
nesmiseln in na smrt grozljiv. Tisto,
kar mi hoče čute raznesti, mi ne da
dihati, nekaj neznosno čistega,
breztelesnega in pretresljivega me
hoče vzdigniti v zrak. Naveličal sem
se vsega obljubljenega, zemeljsko
dobrega in usmiljenega. Vedel sem, da
sem izgubil svojo poslednjo igro,
srditi obračun se je z divjo in sveto
jezo zazrl vame. Sredi julijske polnoči
sem podivjal in tako dolgo skakal po
svojih gugajočih se sencah, dokler se
nisem zrušil na poteptano travo in
hropel vse do osramočenega jutra.

AMOK

No war knows pity
and no peace knows permanence,
victories are worthless
and pacts prevail without love.
I am soothed most by the evening tents
when the brass band strikes up
at the firemen's ball, and after midnight the boys
croon sentimental songs. Then,
just as I am whispering into a girl's ear,
a wild and pitiless force seizes me.
Suddenly I seem enormously strong,
absurd, and mortally dangerous.
The thing that wishes to burst my senses stops
my breath. Something intolerably pure,
incorporeal and thrilling tries
to hoist me into the air. I got fed up
with all the promises, all the pardons
and all earthly virtue. I knew
I had lost my last game,
a wild and holy rage for furious
retribution welled inside me.
In that July midnight
I ran amok and stamped endlessly
on my swaying shadows, then I
collapsed on the trampled grass and
panted till the disgraced morning.

KAJ SMO ISKALI

Ali se še spomnite,
kako smo se zapodili navzgor
in si osvojili strmi breg
in kako si nismo odpočili,
marveč se zaleteli dalje,
ali se spomnite?
Spomnimo se, spomnimo se.

Ali se še spomnite,
kako smo zdrveli na drugi hrib
in ga v naskoku zasedli,
potem pa odvihrali dalje,
povejte, ali se spomnite?
Spomnimo se, dobro se spomnimo.

Povejte še to, ali se spomnite,
kako smo se zagnali na tretjo goro
in se nismo mogli več ustaviti,
kako smo oddivjali naprej, vedno dalje
in nismo več šteli vzpetin,
ali se spomnite?
Spomniva se, spomniva se.

Ali še vesta, mila moja,
kako se je zatem zravnala zemlja
in se je odprla tuja ravnina
in ni bilo nobenega hriba več?
O spomnim se, spomnim se.

In zakaj se mi je jezik zapletel, bratec?
Kaj naj te še vprašam? Kje si?
In koga naj vprašam?
Izgubil sem spomin in ne vem več,
kaj smo iskali.

Do you still remember
how we rushed uphill
and conquered the steep scarp
and how we did not stop to rest
but dashed on,
do you remember?
We remember, we remember.

Do you still remember
how we sprinted up another hill
and took it by assault
and then stormed on,
tell me, do you remember?
We remember, we remember it well.

Tell me if you also remember
how we hurled ourselves up a third mountain
and could no longer stop,
how we stampeded farther and farther,
no longer counting the slopes,
do you remember?
We remember, we both remember.

Do you both still recall, dear friends,
how the land flattened out after that
and a strange plain opened before us
and there were no hills any more?
Oh, I remember, I remember.

So why, brother, does my tongue now stumble?
What else can I ask you? Where have you gone?
And to whom shall I now put my questions?
I have lost my memory, and I no longer know
what we were looking for.

SPOMENIK

Vzdignil je glavo
in jo poslej drži
slovesno od večera do večera,
do tod in nikamor dalje.
Sprožil je nogo za korak
in jo poslej drži vzdignjeno
od jutra do jutra,
do tod in nikamor dalje.

Potem je vzdignil obe roki,
kakor je bilo rečeno,
in ju obdržal razpeti
ves dan in vso noč,
do tod in nikamor dalje.

In tedaj smo čakali
na njegov močni in odrešni glas
ali pa na to, da bi odšel
pred nami pod slavolokom,
kakor je bilo rečeno,
sapa pa se igra okoli njega,
do tod in nikamor dalje.

142

THE STATUE

He raised his head
and has held it there ever since,
solemnly from evening to evening,
thus far and no farther.
He thrust his foot forward
and has since kept it raised
from morning to morning,
thus far and no farther.

Then he lifted both hands
as it was said
and has held them outstretched
all day and all night,
thus far and no farther.

And then we waited
for his mighty and saving voice
or for him to precede us
through the triumphal arch
as it was said,
but the breeze plays around him,
thus far and no farther.

NEKAJ O JEZIKU

Pokaži jezik,
ne skrivaj ga,
iztegni ga do konca,
spači se z njim
in se osmeši,
kakor si dolžan.
Ali pa ga skrij
v goljufiva usta
in ga požri,
da boš mutasto
sebi zvest.
Ali pa ga stisni
po sredini
in ga prekolji
in zarjuj kot zverina,
da boš začel znova
s čistimi glasovi.

TONGUE

Show me your tongue,
don't hide it,
poke it all the way out,
pull a face with it
and make a fool of yourself
as you are bound to do.
Or hide it
in your deceitful mouth
and swallow it
so as to be dumbly
faithful to yourself.
Or maybe clench it
down the middle
and chop it in two
and howl like a beast
so you can start anew
with pure sounds.

● *PROŠNJA*

Mandeljštam pravi, da na književniški
obrti cenimo le še divje meso, blazno
izraslino, tisto, kar ni dovoljeno,
čeprav je zapeljivo in morda celo nujno.

Vsako jutro na tihem pokleknem pred
svoj ubogi papir in vroče prosim
velikega duha, da bi se mi njegove
sanje tudi čez dan nadaljevale.

Da bi mi ostala zunanja podoba divjega
moža, strašnega in tihega, deško dobrega,
preprostega in nadarjenega, z uporabo
vseh osemnajstih barv ljubezenske mavrice.

Predvsem pa, da bi v svoji notranjosti
ostal samemu sebi zvesti Dalaj lama in
da bi se mi resnica razširila v metastazah
in da bi mi koprneči jambor ozelenel.

Mandelstam says that the only thing we prize
in the writer's craft is scar tissue, the crazy
lump, that which is not allowed,
though it's tempting and maybe even necessary.

Each morning I kneel secretly before
my pathetic paper and ardently implore
the great spirit to let his dreams
stay with me throughout the day.

So that I am left with my outer image of a wild
man, terrible and silent, boyishly good,
simple and talented, able to employ
all eighteen colors of love's rainbow.

But above all so I can inwardly remain
a faithful Dalai Lama to myself,
so my truth spawns metastases
and my pining mast turns green.

Jecljajte, otroci, jecljajte,
če že ne morete govoriti od strahu,
jecljajte s hibami jezika, srca
in pameti, laže boste premagovali
težke slutnje, kajti nad vas bodo
prišle hude stvari, hujše, kakor smo
jih doživeli mi sami. Naj vas ne bo sram
strahu, nevednosti in strašne domišljije.

Tisti, ki vam to govorim, imam
od nekdaj zvito oslabljene oči,
sposobne videti stvari v spačenosti
in v ljubeznivi učenosti, ki je
slajša od sramu in varnejša od slepote.
Ko sem nekoč pogledal z glavo
nad ostale glave in na mah pregledal
vso položno stran, sem kradoma zagledal,
da ima vsakdo svoje strašilo in da
prikazni komaj čakajo na svojo uro.
Zato jecljajte, otroci, da vam bo laže.

STAMMER, CHILDREN

Stammer, children, stammer,
if you are afraid to speak more,
stammer with all the defects of language, heart,
and mind, it will be easier for you to overcome
heavy forebodings, for you will encounter
horrible things, worse than we ourselves
experienced. Don't be ashamed
of your fear, ignorance, and terrible imaginings.

I who am telling you this have always had
cunningly weakened eyes
capable of seeing things in all their deformity
and charming erudition, which is
sweeter than shame and safer than blindness.
One day when I looked with my head
over other heads and swiftly observed
the whole sloping side, I stealthily noticed
that everyone has his bogeyman and that
apparitions can hardly wait for their hour to come.
So stammer, children, to make it easier.

DEKLICA

Vsak pomenljivi dan te srečam
in ne vem, odkod datumi.
Odkod praštevila, predvsem liha?
In zakaj me vznemirjaš?
Nič zlomljenega in nič celega.
Le to, da hodiš med nami
izgubljena in razsvetljena,
nevarna plesalka, varna mesečnica,
kar naprej sama in neuničljiva,
zamaknjena v večere in jutra,
s toplimi ovinki v telesu,
s priprtimi mukami pod vekami
in z blaznim psom v svoji senci,
ki te nikoli ne ubrani divjine.

Vsak pomenljivi dan te srečam
in te vedno bolj blagrujem,
vijolica na pikovi sedmici,
krvava rosa prebodenih noči,
smrtno darežljiva milina
z obhajilno svečo v nedrih,
vse ti je vnaprej odpuščeno
kakor vonj sena pred nevihto.
Brezimno omamljena mamilka,
nenasitna čebela divjega medu,
mrtva posiljenka na jasi,
najbolj razširjena rastlina,
ki se je ne napasejo gobci,
neuničljivi mah, lišaj za čaj
na južnem tečaju, sinja slina,
zelena mrena na svetem očesu.

GIRL

Each memorable day I meet you
and I don't know why dates matter.
Why prime numbers, especially odd ones?
And why do you disturb me?
There is nothing broken and nothing whole.
It's just that you walk among us
lost and illuminated,
dangerous dancer, secure moonwalker,
ever alone and indestructible,
rapt in the mornings and evenings,
with warm serpentines in your body,
with lowered torments under your lids
and with a mad dog in your shadow
that never holds the wilderness at bay.

Each memorable day I meet you
and I bless you more and more,
a violet on the seven of spades,
bloody dew of transfixed nights,
fatally generous sweetness
with a communion candle in your bosom,
all is forgiven you beforehand,
like the smell of hay before a storm.
Anonymous intoxicated temptress,
insatiable bee of wild honey,
raped and dead in a clearing,
the commonest plant,
that muzzles can't get enough of,
indestructible moss, lichen for tea
at the south pole, bright blue saliva,
green cataract on the sacred eye.

O SVOBODI UMA

Nočem več lepih stavkov,
ostaja mi ena sama beseda,
ko padem na ležišče, vzkliknem: ne,
in ko sanjam, zakričim nenadoma: ne,
in ko se prebudim, rečem znova: ne.
To je moj način kljubovanja,
dela me zdravega in odpornega.

Kadar sem že utrujen,
še vedno zmorem besedo: ne,
in kadar vsi ponavljajo: da,
se zakrohotam z besedico: ne.
S to besedo obvladam položaj,
to je moj način pritrjevanja,
dela me bistrega in krutega.

Soroden sem koreninam in klicam,
brezobzirnim viharjem in sapam,
trakovi računalnikov se trgajo
ob moji kratki besedi: ne.
Račun se vsakikrat začne znova,
kadar pravijo, da sem kriv,
sem sam iz sebe nedolžen.

Zakon o svobodi človekovega uma
je enak tihi brambi urbarijev,
klovnu je zapoved prepoved,
nočem biti blaznež ali pošast,
postajam hripav sredi strojev,
iz gore v goro devet odmevov: ne,
pri sosedu se slišijo kot: da.

No more fine phrases, please,
one word alone is left for me,
when I lie on the couch I say "no,"
and when I dream I suddenly cry "no,"
and when I wake I again say "no."
That is my form of defiance,
it keeps me healthy and stubborn.

Even when I am tired
I can still say the word "no,"
and when everyone is saying "yes,"
I guffaw that little word "no."
With this word I control the situation,
it's my form of affirmation,
it keeps me clear-headed and cruel.

I am kin to roots and shoots,
to ruthless tempests and breezes,
calculator printouts are shredded
by my brief word, "no."
The calculation always has to begin again,
when they say I am guilty
my actions say I am innocent.

The law of freedom of the human mind
is like the quiet defense of ancient rights;
to the clown a command is a prohibition,
I don't want to be a madman or a monster,
I get hoarse amid the din of machines,
from mountain to mountain I send nine echoes of "no."
My neighbor hears it as "yes."

PRASTARI ČUDEŽ

Prisluhni dogajanju
v moji ubogi glavi,
nekaj tihega in veselega
se snuje med brado in čelom,
česar ne morem videti
pa ga čutim izzivalno,
čeprav ga ne morem izreči,
nekaj, kar slišim,
pa ga ne morem doseči,
nekaj, kar dosežem,
pa ga ne morem doumeti,
nekaj, kar doumem,
pa mi ostaja kar naprej
neodgonetljivo in neznano,
nekaj, kar drhti
in mi greje bose noge
in mi hladi vroče čelo
in ostaja neizbrisen spomin
in bo molčalo na vse veke,
več od skrivnosti
in več od ljubezni,
najgloblje bistvo stvari,
nekaj, za kar ni besede,
kar je srečna nevednost
in blažena slutnja,
nekaj, kar je nenehno
na drugi strani,
pa je vendar v meni.

❧ *ANCIENT MIRACLE*

Listen to what is going on
in my poor head;
something quiet and merry
is being hatched between my brow and my chin,
which I cannot see,
but I can feel it tickling me,
though I cannot say it,
it is something I hear
but cannot reach,
something I reach
but cannot grasp,
something I grasp
but remains forever
indecipherable and unknown,
something that quivers
and warms my bare feet
and cools my hot brow
and remains an indelible memory
and will stay silent forever,
more than a mystery
and more than love,
the deepest essence of things,
something for which there is no word,
which is happy oblivion,
a blessed presentiment,
something constantly
on the other side
but always within me.

DAREŽLJIVOST PESMI

V vseh časih so naročali pesnikom,
naj kot slovesni zgodovinoslovci
skušajo s posebnimi besedami uloviti
spomina vredne usodne človeške dogodke,
da bi se jih stari in mladi naučili
na pamet in jih prepevali za žalost,
v slavo in poduk vsem rodovom. In
glejte, pesniki so se vselej razigrali
in svojo sveto dolžnost do zgodovine
povezali z nezadržano slo po prvinski igri.
Napisali so pesmi kakor dež in sneg
opravita svojo dolžnost v naravi
in kakor marljivi sejavec poseje
zorane njive jeseni in jih poleti požanje.
V tem hipu čutim posebno darežljivost.
Hranjena je iz vsega, kar je bilo
in kar je ostalo v človekovem čaščenju
in presega moj spomin in se spaja z vsem,
kar živi z občestvom in z domišljijo.
Zdaj čutim, kakor tega še nisem, da je
pesem strnjena sila vseh človekovih
sposobnosti in da je njena vzornost
v presežnosti jezika.

Poets throughout the ages, like solemn historians,
have been commanded to capture with special words
those fateful human accidents worth remembering,
so that old and young may learn them
by heart, and sing them in sorrow,
as a celebration and a lesson for the generations. But
you see, poets have always gotten carried away
and combined their sacred duty toward history
with an unstoppable lust for primitive play.
They have written their poems the way rain and snow
do their duty to nature,
the way the patient laborer sows the plowed field
in fall and harvests it the following summer.
But just now I feel a special generosity.
It is nourished by everything that ever was
and has remained in human worship
and overflows my memory and fuses with all things
that dwell in community and fantasy.
I feel now, as never before, that
a poem is the condensed power of all human
abilities, and that its ideal lies
in the power of language to transcend itself.

ZDAJ SVA SAMA

Iz ključev vrata,
strop iz temen,
stopala iz blata,
vrt iz semen,
iz oči zrelišče,
iz vzdihov ležišče.

Izglajena raba,
romanje snovi,
spomin in pozaba
in vse, kar trpi,
je čista omama,
kadar sva sama.

Pred spočetjem nič
in po smrti mrlič,
najin prepad
en sam prosti pad
v brezdanjo skrivnost
in nad njo most.

Doors made of keys,
ceiling of skulls,
feet of clay,
garden of semen,
horizon of eyes,
couch of sighs.

Smoothed custom,
the pilgrimage of things,
memory and oblivion,
and all that stings
end in a pure swoon
when we are alone.

Before conception we are nothing,
after death—a corpse,
this abyss of ours
is a free fall
into a bottomless pit,
over it is a bridge.

IGRA

Vedno bolj se bliža,
vedno bolj se niža,
kar miruje in kar neti
starodavna viža,
vse slasti in strašne muke,
elektronke, stare kljuke,
kar je zgoraj in je spodaj,
kar je skrito in očito,
kar je sveto in prekleto,
kar je bolno, kar je zdravo,
šepetanje, tulba, govorica,
sunek z nogo in poljub na lica,
kar je lažno, kar je verno,
kar jutranje, kar večerno,
kar je jasno, kar je motno,
kar je zmotno in popotno,
nevsiljivo, brezobzirno,
bojevito, večno mirno,
kar se bliža, vedno bolj se bliža,
kar je nova viža, to je stara viža,
naj nas babica prekriža.

GAME

Closer and closer again,
lower and lower again,
all that's quietened and all that's kindled
by that old refrain.
All the delights and terrible torments,
electric valves and ancient latches,
all that's up and all that's down,
all that's hidden and all that's exposed
all that's holy and all that's damned,
all that's sickly and all that's sound,
whispers, murmurs and hissing,
not to mention kicking and kissing,
all that's false and all that's faithful,
all that's nocturnal and also matutinal,
all that's clear and all that's cloudy,
all that's wrong and still traveling,
that's unobtrusive, indestructible,
still pugnacious or even peaceable,
all that's coming is coming closer again,
new refrains are the same old refrain,
grandmother, bless us all.

❧ NISEM SE DOVOLJ NAIGRAL Z BESEDAMI

Nisem se dovolj naigral z besedami,
ki nosijo smisel, zdaj bi se rad predal
nevarni igri besed, ki nič ne pomenijo
in so same sebi skrivnost. Svoboda je
straššna svoboda niča. Na katero
stran bom stopil zdaj, ko je nastopil
skrajni čas. Doslej sem se igral, poslej
bom skrit v zemlji izgovarjal
neznane besede skozi eone, morda
vso večnost (. . .)

I haven't done playing with words
that have meaning, now I would like to give myself up
to the dangerous game of words that mean nothing
and are a mystery to themselves. Freedom is
the terrible freedom of nothingness. Which side
shall I choose now that the decisive moment
has come? Till now I have played, but from now on,
hidden in the earth, I shall utter
unknown words through the eons, perhaps
through all eternity . . .

Kocbek was working on this unfinished poem at the time of his death in 1981.

THE LOCKERT LIBRARY OF POETRY IN TRANSLATION

George Seferis: Collected Poems (1924–1995), translated, edited, and introduced by Edmund Keeley and Philip Sherrard

Collected Poems of Lucio Piccolo, translated and edited by Brian Swann and Ruth Feldman

C. P. Cavafy: Selected Poems, translated by Edmund Keeley and Philip Sherrard and edited by George Savidis

Benny Andersen: Collected Poems, translated by Alexander Taylor

Selected Poetry of Andrea Zanzotto, edited and translated by Ruth Feldman and Brian Swann

Poems of René Char, translated and annotated by Mary Ann Caws and Jonathan Griffin

Selected Poems of Tudor Arghezi, translated by Michael Impey and Brian Swann

"The Survivor" and Other Poems by Tadeusz Różewicz, translated and introduced by Magnus J. Krynski and Robert A. Maguire

"Harsh World" and Other Poems by Angel González, translated by Donald D. Walsh

Ritsos in Parentheses, translations and introduction by Edmund Keeley

Salamander: Selected Poems of Robert Marteau, translated by Anne Winters

Angelos Sikelianos: Selected Poems, translated and introduced by Edmund Keeley and Philip Sherrard

Dante's "Rime," translated by Patrick S. Diehl

Selected Later Poems of Marie Luise Kaschnitz, translated by Lisel Mueller

Osip Mandelstam's "Stone," translated and introduced by Robert Tracy

The Dawn Is Always New: Selected Poetry of Rocco Scotellaro, translated by Ruth Feldman and Brian Swann

Sounds, Feelings, Thoughts: Seventy Poems by Wisława Szymborska, translated and introduced by Magnus J. Krynski and Robert A. Maguire

The Man I Pretend to Be: "The Colloquies" and Selected Poems of Guido Gozzano, translated and edited by Michael Palma, with an introductory essay by Eugenio Montale

D'Après Tout: Poems by Jean Follain, translated by Heather McHugh

Songs of Something Else: Selected Poems of Gunnar Ekelöf, translated by Leonard Nathan and James Larson

The Little Treasury of One Hundred People, One Poem Each, compiled by Fujiwara No Sadaie and translated by Tom Galt

The Ellipse: Selected Poems of Leonardo Sinisgalli, translated by W. S. Di Piero

The Difficult Days by Roberto Sosa, translated by Jim Lindsey

Hymns and Fragments by Friedrich Hölderlin, translated and introduced by Richard Sieburth

The Silence Afterwards: Selected Poems of Rolf Jacobsen, translated and edited by Roger Greenwald

Rilke: Between Roots, selected poems rendered from the German by Rika Lesser

In the Storm of Roses: Selected Poems by Ingeborg Bachmann, translated, edited, and introduced by Mark Anderson

Birds and Other Relations: Selected Poetry of Dezsö Tandori, translated by Bruce Berlind

Brocade River Poems: Selected Works of the Tang Dynasty Courtesan Xue Tao, translated and introduced by Jeanne Larsen

The True Subject: Selected Poems of Faiz Ahmed Faiz, translated by Naomi Lazard

My Name on the Wind: Selected Poems of Diego Valeri, translated by Michael Palma

Aeschylus: The Suppliants, translated by Peter Burian

Foamy Sky: The Major Poems of Miklós Radnóti, selected and translated by Zsuzsanna Ozváth and Frederick Turner

La Fontaine's Bawdy: Of Libertines, Louts, and Lechers, translated by Norman R. Shapiro

A Child Is Not a Knife: Selected Poems of Göran Sonnevi, translated and edited by Rika Lesser

George Seferis: Collected Poems, Revised Edition, translated, edited, and introduced by Edmund Keeley and Philip Sherrard

C. P. Cavafy: Collected Poems, Revised Edition, translated and introduced by Edmund Keeley and Philip Sherrard, and edited by George Savidis

Selected Poems of Shmuel HaNagid, translated from the Hebrew by Peter Cole

The Late Poems of Meng Chiao, translated and introduced by David Hinton

Leopardi: Selected Poems, translated and introduced by Eamon Gennan

Through Naked Branches: Selected Poems of Tarjei Vesaas, translated and edited by Roger Greenwald

The Complete Odes and Satires of Horace, translated with introduction and notes by Sidney Alexander

Selected Poems of Solomon Ibn Gabirol, translated by Peter Cole

Puerilities: Erotic Epigrams of The Greek Anthology, translated by Daryl Hine

Night Journey by María Negroni, translated and introduced by Anne Twitty

Nothing Is Lost: Selected Poems by Edvard Kocbek, translated by Michael Scammell and Veno Taufer, and introduced by Michael Scammell